An Unexpected Life

DEBRA CHWAST PAINTINGS BY SETH CHWAST
PREFACE BY SEYMOUR CHWAST

An Unexpected Life

A Mother and Son's Story
of LOVE, DETERMINATION,
AUTISM, and ART

STERLING
New York

KH

STERLING
New York

An Imprint of Sterling Publishing
387 Park Avenue South
New York, NY 10016

Book design and layout: Christine Heun
All artwork photography courtesy of Fuchs & Kasperek Inc.

ISBN 978-1-4027-7403-4

Library of Congress Cataloging-in-Publication Data

Chwast, Debra.
  An unexpected life : speaking through art / Debra Chwast with Seth Chwast.
    p. cm.
  Includes bibliographical references and index.
  ISBN 978-1-4027-7403-4 (alk. paper)
  1. Chwast, Seth. 2. Chwast, Debra. 3. Autistic children--United States--Biography. 4.
Autistic artists--United States--Biography. 5. Autistic children--Education--United States--
Case studies. 6. Painting--Study and teaching--United States--Case studies. 7. Art therapy-
-United States--Case studies. 8. Mother and child--United States--Case studies. I. Chwast,
Seth. II. Title.
  RJ506.A9C483 2011
  616.85'8820092--dc22
  [B]
                                                                          2010046453

Distributed in Canada by Sterling Publishing
^{c}/o Canadian Manda Group, 165 Dufferin Street
Toronto, Ontario, Canada M6K 3H6
Distributed in the United Kingdom by GMC Distribution Services
Castle Place, 166 High Street, Lewes, East Sussex, England BN7 1XU
Distributed in Australia by Capricorn Link (Australia) Pty. Ltd.
P.O. Box 704, Windsor, NSW 2756, Australia

For information about custom editions, special sales, and premium and corporate purchases,
please contact Sterling Special Sales at 800-805-5489 or specialsales@sterlingpublishing.com.

Manufactured in China

2 4 6 8 10 9 7 5 3 1

3/6/12

To my mother, Sandra Louise Hilda Newmark, who loved family, beauty, fun, music, drama, and art.

To my father, Milton J. Newmark, who always persevered, never gave up, and enjoyed life to the last minute.

To my son, Seth, who fills me with joy.

Contents

I am a graphic designer, illustrator, and painter with two autistic grandsons. My connection with Seth came through our same, though rare, last name, and I realized that we were related. Debra knew my work and thought I'd be interested in seeing the work of her son. What I saw amazed me—his work has exuberant color, form, and creative imagination with a range and output on a par with any other working artist.

Debra Chwast is a remarkable woman who credits Seth for her "endurance and perseverance." She has had a lot more than a mom's drive for success for her child. In this case it is a son with extreme challenges and a mom with total determination for his achieving that success.

Seth is not constrained by a necessity to direct his work. (As an illustrator that is my foremost duty.) He can act on anything that inspires him. The results cover a wide range from turtles, hippocampuses, and horses to abstract work, self-portraits, flowers, and buildings. The work covers the conceptual to the decorative; from impressionism to expressionism to minimalism; from his sense of realism to imaginative fantasy. He indulges in experimentation—as the professionals call it—to justify narrowly focused work.

Seth's genre, called self-taught or outsider art, is recognized by critics, museums, and collectors. The artists come from everywhere but do not have formal training. They have, however, the same or greater urge to creative as learned ones. They operate in a different universe from the rest of us but have a vision that shows us a world that is unique—but still a part of the human condition.

I don't know if Seth realizes the importance of his body of work. In the end his paintings leave him "excited," as he tells us, while the rest of us get caught up in his fascination with the act of creating art.

In their book *American Self-Taught*, Roger Ricco and Frank Maresca said, "Self-taught images constantly remind us that art does not mirror some established reality but instead illuminates experience. Arising from no specific milieu but underlying all the works is the artists' drive to testify fully to his or her circumstance."

The creative urge is a mystery. I don't know what part of the brain or nervous system provokes me to make something that has never been seen before. In Seth's case, acting on his creative urge was not a conscious method of advancing a career or satisfying an ego. It is for him the way for anyone with a vision . . . the thing they have to do. I look back to paintings and drawings I've done that were not commissioned. While I am glad they were done (and many were just bad) I have to admire and be curious about the incentive within me that got me to create the work.

Seth is artistic and autistic. The special talent that some of those similarly affected have belong to all of us to admire, absorb and love.

Seymour Chwast

INTRODUCTION

Dreams

No parents ever imagine that their child will be autistic. During pregnancy, shadows of worry flit through dreams of a healthy, happy, and whole child but they dissolve quickly in the bright light of day. You don't dwell on what you can't imagine.

I know I never imagined that I would have an autistic son. I never imagined that he would be evaluated for a career in dry mopping at age eighteen. I never imagined that he would start to paint at twenty, and by twenty-three become a successful painter of huge, colorful canvases and be featured on the *Today* show as an artist. Now, at twenty-eight, he paints daily, has art exhibitions, speaks through his paintings, and lives in a state of bliss. I never imagined any of this for my son, but I've discovered, after nearly two decades of struggle, that it was my imagination that was lacking—not my son's. Not Seth's.

My life before Seth included growing up in Brooklyn, a degree in social work from the University of California at Berkeley, marriage, and living in Manhattan. Life was full and exciting; it seemed as though there was never enough time to do all that my husband and I wanted to do. Living in New York City felt like one wonderful experience after another—foreign films, plays, and dance performances kept us busy as we discovered all that the city had to offer. After a few years of city life, we moved to Cleveland, Ohio. While my husband pursued his PhD in psychology at Case Western Reserve University, I enrolled in the Gestalt Institute, studied with Masters and Johnson, and began studying medical hypnosis. Meanwhile, our idyllic life continued. We traveled the world: Iceland, Greenland, Kenya, Uganda, Ethiopia, Greece, Turkey, Bulgaria, Madeira, Lapland, Scandinavia, and more.

OPPOSITE: Detail, *Rocket Man 2*, 2008. Oil on canvas, 30 × 48 inches.

1

The world was ours to explore and we were free to go where our wanderlust took us.

When I turned thirty, however, I realized something was missing. Up until this point we hadn't considered having a child in our lives. When the need hit, it hit hard and unexpectedly. I remember the moment vividly. While on vacation in Vermont, I was standing in the shower and as the water washed over me, I was suddenly flooded with the desire for a child. I felt compelled to become a link in the chain of motherhood that extended to me from my mother and my grandmother and beyond. I wanted a baby.

Sometimes the things we want don't come as easily as we hope. That moment in the shower was followed by five years of trying to conceive. Suddenly our life was filled with infertility clinics and carefully planned sex. Forget January, February, March, et cetera; the only calendar I knew was the ovulation calendar. There would be a week of waiting, then a week of trying, followed by a week of hope, ending in a week of disappointment. And then it would start all over again. Finally, it happened. I was pregnant. To say that I was overjoyed is an understatement. We were over the moon. I don't think my husband or I stopped grinning for weeks after we found out. It was such a relief to be free of trying. We had waited so long it hardly seemed real. I was carrying a secret that I couldn't yet share with the world. Many times a day my hand strayed to my belly, and as many women do, I imagined my future child and all that he could be. The dreams I held for him were boundless.

Nine months later I was at a Seder, sitting on towels in case my water broke. At 10:30 p.m. I announced, "I want to go to the hospital!" Waves of pain and excitement coursed through me as we rushed toward our child's birth. Although I was told I was in early labor and that it would be two or three days until I delivered, I wouldn't leave the hospital.

Introduction: Dreams

"I'm not going anywhere until this baby is born!" I firmly told the nurse.

They reluctantly gave me a bed. My husband massaged my back to keep me comfortable, and I waited nervously for what would happen next. When the nurse came by to check on me, I asked for a change of sheets because mine were wet (I hadn't realized my water broke). She took a look, shouted "The baby is coming!," and ran to get the doctor. A short time later, and with relatively no pain, Seth was born.

I was in love. The beginning was pure bliss. I don't know how many times I counted his tiny fingers and toes or traced the curve of his sweet cheek. I could look at him all day and marvel at the miracle of my boy.

When Seth was seven months old, I wrote in his baby book:

You are absorbed in your world. You study the tiniest speck, move the heaviest pillows, reach for the highest shelves. You seem wonderfully in control. You started crawling at four months, by seven months you are fast. Now you stand by yourself and walk all over if we hold both hands. You never fall down. When you practice standing, it ends in a plop-down, not a fall. You are sunny, not very clingy, maybe not even cuddly. You enjoy us, but you are busy taking on the world. You are always going. Not hyper, not wild, but busy, intense, watching, exploring. Your concentration is fantastic. You spend a long time on one activity. If we distract you, you remember what you were doing and go back to it. You are easy, reasonable, comfortable with life, the world, yourself. You are outgoing and curious.

Several weeks later I wrote:

At eight months you took your first step alone. By nine months you are walking alone full speed ahead. Your favorite activity is watching Sesame Street. Your favorite song is the Mickey Mouse Club's

"Mickey Mouse." Your favorite books are Pat the Bunny and Where Is Spot? Your favorite toys are blocks, Duplo [the baby version of Lego], and puzzles.

Were there clues? Signs? Was he a little remote? All I saw was an easygoing, curious baby. When did I start to think something was wrong? It came in bits and pieces. When Seth was over a year old, we were in a playgroup with about five or six moms and their babies. One day I was talking to Seth like I always did, and another mom said, "Wow! Can he understand that?" I realized they were using simple sentences when they spoke to their kids and their children understood what they were saying. I was chatting away to Seth without thinking about his comprehension or response, figuring that he'd respond sooner or later. Later seemed to never come.

Motherhood was very consuming, and I was also working in my private practice as a clinical social worker. My days were full; I was tired but happy.

One day when Seth was fourteen months old, we were visiting a zoo. A rooster crowed right next to us, but Seth didn't react. His lack of response to loud sounds and his lack of speech except for the occasional word made us wonder if he could be deaf. We had his hearing tested at sixteen months . . . and all the results were normal. I wanted normal, I hoped for normal, and I prayed for normal, yet something wasn't right. Perhaps my vision of him was clouded because I had waited so long for this child. I loved him so much. Really, Seth didn't seem much different from other children. In fact, his attention span seemed developed beyond his age. He watched *Sesame Street* for hours. The problem was language. Seth said "Mama" at ten months and "Dada" at twelve months. Then he lost all language until fifteen months when he said, "Hi," and "Up." At eighteen and a half months he loved to recite the letters A through G and numbers one through nine. I thought it was funny and charming that one of his first words was *octagon*. Yet he wasn't babbling or chatting or making lots of sounds. He barely spoke at all.

Our world changed in 1985, after our annual New Year's Eve party. Because my husband was a psychologist and I was a social worker, many of our guests were friends in similar fields. The day after our party, a friend, a child psychologist, called. I thought she was calling to say thanks for the party or that she had left something behind. I was completely unprepared for what came next.

"Debra, I think there is something wrong with Seth."

I felt chilled. I could barely choke out, "What do you mean?"

The world fell away as I waited for her to speak again. "I think he is autistic."

I wanted to shout, You're wrong! It cannot be. This is my baby we're talking about! I don't remember the rest of the conversation. I wanted to scream, to run, to cry. I got off the phone as fast as I could and ran to where Seth sat on the floor. I picked him up in a bear hug—he wriggled out of my arms and went back to what he was doing.

Seth was twenty-one months old. Hearing her pronouncement about our bright, wonderful child, I couldn't breathe. When I finally caught my breath, my husband and I had a long conversation about Seth that went deep into the night. In my heart, I knew there must be a kernel of truth in what she said about Seth. What were we to do? Finally, we called another dear friend, Nick Krawiecki, a pediatric neurologist in Atlanta. He recommended a specialist who could evaluate Seth. After a session with Seth, the specialist told us that he might have agnosia, the inability to recognize familiar things. Apparently, agnosia is worse than autism—a lot worse. I was scared. My dreams for my little boy started to die. Life became a blur. In a daze, we started language therapy and music therapy. We had to do something to help our son.

Several weeks later we flew to New York for a neurological evaluation and EEG at Albert Einstein College of Medicine. I hoped against hope that somehow everyone was wrong and the neurologist would tell us that everything was okay, that Seth was okay. Nothing prepared me for the moment when the doctor said, "Dr. and Mrs. Chwast, our evaluation shows that Seth is autistic." It was official. The thing that I had resisted the most was now true. I was terrified of the word autism, with its connotation of kids who were remote and distant. Because autism seemed such a dire diagnosis I preferred aphasia, which means the inability to decode or produce language. It was certainly true that Seth didn't seem able to process or produce language. Others weren't so reluctant to label Seth. Our neurologist was sure that Seth was autistic. She also pointed out that there was funding for research and treatment for autism. If I insisted on *aphasia* and wouldn't use *autism*, she warned, my son would not get the help he needed. I wasn't really worried about giving him help—we already had Seth lined up for language therapy and music therapy, each twice a week.

"It's not enough," the neurologist told us. She said he needed hours of help, and multiple therapies, every day. If we moved to New York and entered their program at Einstein, it was possible that he might make gains in language and catch up to other children by age five. But my husband was still in graduate school and we had just bought a home in Cleveland, so it felt like too much, on top of such a life-changing diagnosis, for us to move to New York.

We returned to Ohio and enrolled Seth at a special needs nursery school, about forty-five minutes from our home. His dad drove Seth there every morning, waited two hours until class was over, then drove him home. The music and language therapy also continued. Additionally, we were provided with a tutor and chose a psychologist to help us. Seth was having a wide range of therapies and interventions, and I could still not accept that he was autistic. I used the autism label to get him services but I refused to accept the diagnosis. In fact, it would be years before I could actually say that Seth was autistic.

Why did I fight the label? It was 1985. When I called a top therapist in the field, she said she would see me three times a week. And Seth? How often would she see Seth? There was silence. Then she replied, "Haven't you asked yourself why your child doesn't speak?"

These were the days of "refrigerator moms," who supposedly caused autism. The inability to speak was a cry for help from children with cold, distant moms—moms so uncaring that their children were damaged for life. Because of the moms, the theory went, the autistic children were remote, detached, and uncaring. This was not our reality. Yet my son did not speak.

We were catapulted on a journey we didn't anticipate or want, which seemed like a nightmare. Our dreams and hopes were shattered. Everything we expected was over. Nothing prepared us for this—not other people's pain and stories—*nothing*. We were incredulous. We wondered, *How could this happen to us?* It's too hard, too bleak, and too unfair.

Seth would not be like other people. He would not wake up one day and be able to speak normally. He would never be independent. He would not be able to protect himself. The words *never, won't, unable*, and *can't* swirled around my son. Life did not give me a "normal" kid, but I knew that I would do all that was in my power to give him the best life he could possibly have.

The dream changed.

seth chwast

09-26-06

CHAPTER 1
The Blues and Other Colors

Nothing prepares you for having a child with a disability.

I was depressed, overwhelmed, and confused. I wanted to know what the future held for my son. While it was impossible to predict, it was looking rather bleak. Our psychologist said, yes, there were kids who just turned around and were fine, but more often than not they continued to have problems.

I called my parents nightly. I couldn't stop crying. One night my dad said, "Seth is a person, not a statistic; we have to wait and see what will happen." I continued to sob.

My mother was equally supportive. "We'll stand by you and help you in any way we can," she told me, "no matter what." Although I wasn't in this alone, it was hard to calm down.

Every night, Seth and I watched *Dumbo*. In it, Dumbo, who has oversized ears, never speaks. Mrs. Jumbo loves him; she adores him; she wants to protect him. Dumbo had his ears. Seth didn't talk. It sounds odd, but I felt that Mrs. Jumbo and I had a lot in common. From then on *Dumbo* became our movie.

The world said Seth was autistic. My heart told me he was joyful, creative, and fun-loving. I knew he was much more than a diagnosis. But no matter what I thought, we still had to get Seth educated in a way deemed appropriate for an autistic child. Schools became a major issue. After attending the special needs nursery school forty-five minutes away, we enrolled Seth in a preschool that was close by—those were relatively good years.

At age six, Seth was accepted into a Montessori school. The topic for the year was geography. Seth excelled in making maps of America.

OPPOSITE: *Self Study 09-26-06*, 2006. Graphite with acrylic wash on paper, 24 × 18 inches.

When he finished the map of North America (the only child in the class to do so), he went on to make maps of Europe, Asia, South America, and Africa. He loved the map of United States, and he knew the capital of every state. He could look at flash cards and name every state by shape. (I always say Seth doesn't talk, and then I report things he's said. Seth has speech but not functional language. He can express himself but has trouble with the back and forth of a conversation.) He had flash cards for the flags of ninety countries and could match them perfectly. At the end of the year, however, he was not invited back. In his mapping, memory, and drawing skills he was well ahead of every child in his group. He just happened not to talk.

From there Seth went to a public school, where he was put in a program for students with severe language problems. We ran into some difficulties when they refused to allow Seth's service dog or nanny/aide into the school. After several meetings, it was determined that Seth, the dog, and his nanny would be welcome at a different public school, and he spent the next three years there.

Seth went from school to school and program to program, and it became clear that he was not moving beyond his autism. As the world seemed to increasingly reject Seth, my admiration for him only grew. I felt he was smarter than I was. I was in awe of his skill with geography. Even today you can name any state and ask Seth what states surround it and he will call out the answers without pausing. Seth was smart. He was gentle. He never hurt anyone. He never broke anything. He was loving. In his first two years, Seth was curious and wonderfully mobile. He seemed more interested in exploring the world than snuggling up. But the years after that he became more physically affectionate. He loved to sit on laps, stay close, and cuddle. His behavior made it very hard for me to believe he was autistic. Weren't kids with autism remote and disconnected from other people? My son had profound difficulties with speech and language, but he cuddled with us and our friends—in fact he was the last of the children in our circle who continued to be affectionate and cuddly as an older child. He loved Legos, and by the time he was eight, he was doing Lego constructions intended for fourteen-year-olds. When those became too easy, he stopped playing with them. I'd struggle to read the blueprint of a Lego rocket or space station and to find one right piece, while he'd glance at the blueprint, upside down, and put together a whole section. He could amaze me in the things he could do, and break my heart over the things he couldn't.

We did everything we could to bring Seth into the larger world. When he was four, we signed up for every subscription available in children's theater, music, and dance. I remember the time I took him to a matinee performance of *The Nutcracker* at the Palace Theatre in Cleveland. Seth heard the opening bars of the piece, and being musical, friendly, and oblivious to social conventions, he started to spell out the letters of the words *the nutcracker* in a conversational tone—"t-h-e-n-u-t-c-r." Before he could finish, we were asked to leave. It was the beginning of the performance and we stood out, so we were escorted from the theater. The manager met us at the exit and offered to watch Seth while I watched the performance. I replied, "Are you out of your mind? Do you think I want to see *The Nutcracker* for the eighth time? I only came so he could see it!" She was polite and tried to be nice to us, asking what would keep Seth quiet. I said, "Maybe food." So we bought him some red licorice and went back in and watched the performance. Seth was mesmerized. We stayed until the end and Seth behaved better than most of the other children, who, by the second half of the performance, were whispering, squirming, and having meltdowns.

That same year his father and I took him to see the dance company Pilobolus. This time there were no children in the audience. It was very quiet. I thought Seth would really enjoy the performance, and he did.

But in the middle of a dance he announced in a loud voice, "Benjamin not in Guatemala." (We did want him to talk, right?) Benjamin is the son of our Atlanta friends Nick and Lis. We had visited the family the previous year for a New Year's Eve celebration, but Benjamin had been in Guatemala. Seth knew that this year when we visited, Benjamin would be there. I don't know what made him think of Benjamin at that moment. The prospect of seeing Benjamin made Seth happy, so he announced it. Seth's dad was upset and wanted to leave because he felt it was unfair to the audience if Seth became a disruption to the performance. But as we were preparing to go, someone tapped me on the shoulder. We turned around and saw Wendy, a waitress from Seth's favorite restaurant, Lopez, who whispered, "No, stay. Don't leave. He'll be fine." We stayed. He was fine.

We wanted Seth to learn to be comfortable in restaurants. Lopez was a Mexican restaurant near us that we all liked and we'd often go there for a meal. Yreka, Seth's service dog, went along, quietly lying under the table the entire time. We happened to be assigned to Wendy's station one night, and when she came to take our order, she told us she had waited six months to get us and the dog. After that, we always asked for one of her tables.

MY DREAM—THE ONLY HAPPY ENDING I could imagine for Seth—was that we'd work really hard to help Seth's brain compensate and he would start to talk. But when he turned twelve, it finally sunk in that it just wasn't going to happen. Reality had slowly worn away the dream, and somehow the grief left with it. I felt numb. I couldn't think out of the box long enough to wonder if there could be a different kind of happy ending for him. I loved Seth. I cherished him. But perhaps love wasn't enough. By now I understood that our world was going to be a continuation of what it had been for the first twelve years: therapy, more therapy, special schools, disappointments, gains, losses. We would not be like other families, ever.

As much as I wanted Seth to get an education, I did not see where school was taking us. All his therapists were pulling him along inch by inch toward being the best he could be. I loved them and valued them for their work with Seth. But he was not going to end up at college or in a functional language situation or even in independent living. He was not going to end up anywhere I had imagined. If I couldn't get Seth a normal life, I decided to shoot for happiness.

In truth, I was hoping for more than happiness. I was hoping for a way for Seth to shine and grow and express his talents. We tried everything—ice skating, horseback riding, music, science experiments, baking, cake decorating, gift wrapping, and books on code breaking. Seth was excellent at breaking codes—could it give him a life? A career? Later we tried computer-assisted design (CAD). We did all we could to find him a career.

At eighteen, Seth had a formal vocational evaluation that determined he was best suited to a career in dry mopping. There we were in the dusty little office where Seth had just completed a three-day evaluation to determine his potential for employment. All that work, all those therapies, all the hours that we and others had devoted to him— with all that he could do, the result was dry mopping? I said I would die first. I walked away from that office knowing that I couldn't let the conventional world define who and what Seth could be or do. I knew he could do something more creative and inventive. Something that was as unique as I knew he was. I wouldn't give up. I was determined to try and try until I could find something Seth could do. If I failed, then he would play Nintendo and take trips to ride roller coasters, or do whatever gave him pleasure. Whatever it was, it would have to give him a good life. So far, breaking codes was our best bet.

In search of enhancing Seth's life experiences, we took him out of school frequently for traveling and spending time with his grandfather. I felt a little guilty about his missing school, but it seemed better to let him see the world than to expect him to fit into it when it didn't seem to have a place for him. Eventually, there was no more school for Seth. At the end of the academic year that a person turns twenty-one, the school system ends its responsibility. So in June 2003 we were on our own. No more language therapy, support staff, or safe havens. All parents dread this moment. I intensified my efforts. We had to find Seth a life.

That summer, Seth and Becky, one of his student mentors, went to a four-session outdoor oil painting class, a one-day charcoal class, and a four-session still life oil class, all at the Cleveland Museum of Art. Seth's first experiments with oils were unexpectedly sophisticated. The students were given an assignment to paint anything they liked. Many of them depicted the museum building, one of the statues in the sculpture garden, or the museum's lagoon. Seth painted *The Post Lamp Streetlights*, which looked like clusters of lanterns from the 1900s. They were what caught his eye and he created something that was beautiful and different from what the other students chose to do. In his charcoal class, Seth's use of charcoal was sophisticated and evocative. In his oil painting class, Seth painted *The Golden Building with Trees Have Autumn Leaves*. Next came *Two Squashes on the Blanket*—one yellow, one orange—with a compelling use of color and texture. A friend who is an artist and an architect looked at his paintings and thought they were impressive. I thought they were terrific, too, but I'm his mom so what do I know? Nevertheless, art seemed to be something Seth was enjoying. In the spirit of following his happiness, I put up signs at the Cleveland Institute of Art, looking for artist mentors. I heard from Donna, a mature woman

ABOVE LEFT: *The Postlamp Streetlights*, 2003. Oil on canvas panel, 16 × 20 inches.

ABOVE RIGHT: *The Golden Building with Trees Have Autumn Leaves*, 2003. Oil on canvas, 16 × 20 inches.

LEFT: *Two Squashes on the Blanket*, 2003. Oil on canvas panel, 16 × 20 inches.

and a photographer who mentored Cleveland Institute of Art (CIA) fifth-year students working on their senior projects. She came, looked at Seth's art, and said she wanted the job.

The day Seth and Donna drove off to the art supply store is the day our lives changed. She had never worked with anyone with special needs, but she didn't ask for help in communicating with Seth. Their relationship sometimes reminded me of the relationship between Annie Sullivan and Helen Keller. Donna let Seth feel brushes in his hand and then choose the ones he liked. She let him choose colors and canvas sizes. Maybe they "spoke art." Who knows? They went off together to the art store and never looked back.

In a typical painting session with Donna, Seth announced, "I need help."

Donna responded by asking him questions, "You always draw the horse facing right. Could you draw it facing left?"

Seth replied, "Grow your brain." When he said this, he made a quick gesture with his forefinger, moving from the top right of his head

Big Red Fantasy Horse, 2004. Oil on canvas, 70 × 84 inches.

The Red Fantasy Horse has Hooves, Mane, Tail & Lips. Sand, Grass & Snow-Capped Mountains. The Horse feels happy.

seth chwast

02-24-06

Tiny Fantasy Walking Horses, 2006. Acrylic on wood, 24 × 24 inches.

There are over 100 Fantasy Horses. There are about 830 Horses. I worked on this Painting for about 1 year. The Horses are Red, Cobalt Blue, Butterscotch & Orange. I did a Large Red Fantasy Horse in 2004. I wanted to do the other 3 colors. I did Cobalt Blue for the *Today* show starting November 15, 2006. I did the Orange Horse for the Plain Dealer in 2007. I will do a Butterscotch Horse.

upward into the air as high as his hand could go, as if indicating what his larger brain would look like. Then he said again, "I need help."

Donna asked him, "Where will you start? Where do you want the head?"

I've watched Seth start his paintings in different ways. He drew *Big Red Fantasy Horse* in charcoal as a single line, never stopping and never hesitating. When he finished drawing the body of the horse, he stepped back, looked at what he'd drawn, then made the head larger and went on to draw the desert, hills, mountains, and clouds. In about two minutes he had a 70-by-84-inch sketch. That was a quick painting.

Another early painting is *Tiny Fantasy Walking Horses*, 24 by 24 inches. It took over a year. Seth says, "More than one hundred horses." I tried counting them once and gave up at 720.

Seth can paint many hours a day. While he paints he hums—a sign of bliss. Often he stops and does high kicks, jumping up and down in

seth chwast

ABOVE: *Fantasy Griffin #1 with Purple and Lavender Wings,* 2006.
Oil on canvas,
36 × 60 inches.

Griffin is a Half Eagle, Half Lion. Griffon is a Roller Coaster at Busch Gardens Europe that will be built in Summer 2007. I love Roller Coasters. I like to ride Roller Coasters starting in 1994. I like to paint Skies. I like Griffins in the Sky. I used Different-ent Colors. I made Arms, & Legs like an Eagle. I made Gold Talons. I used many Blues, Purples, & Lavenders are in the Sky.

place, smiling and clapping. Sometimes he gets so excited that he runs down the hall and back. One time he worked on *Big Red Orange Fantasy Horse* all day and *Fantasy Griffin #1 with Purple and Lavender Wings* all evening. He loves to paint!

Seth enjoys his mentors. He has yet to paint or sketch when he is alone. He started with Becky and Donna and then a never-ending stream of art therapists and professional artists who guide, teach, and help him as he paints. We usually work with four or five artists who come at various times and Seth loves their company. They provide social contact as well as instruction.

Every day Seth amazes me with the work he does. I cannot believe the color and grace that pour out of him. I love to watch him paint. In the outside world, Seth has trouble with language. He misses social cues. He can't cross the street on his own. But when it comes to color, he is certain, bold, and comfortable. When he started *Big Red Orange Fantasy Horse*, I was entranced. It touched my heart. I couldn't take my eyes off it. A red-orange horse! Earlier paintings of horses, such as *Big Red Fantasy Horse*, had blue skies with white clouds. Each of these paintings is 5 feet 10 inches by 7 feet. The horses are almost life-size. They feel like family members—they show up in my dreams. As he was painting the red-orange horse, I fell in love with it. And then he started to make pink clouds. Not my kind of rosy pink. Not a pink that I would love, but a bubblegum pink. I went nuts. I felt he was ruining the painting. Donna threw me out of the room. She said, "It's his painting. You have to trust him. It will look better when the grass is in. And he's not finished with the pink." So I left them to the painting. The next morning, when I saw *Big Red Orange Fantasy Horse*, there it was, an incredibly exquisite painting. I stared at the pink clouds and actually loved the painting even more than I had before. It was perfect. White clouds wouldn't have worked as well as the pink ones. Seth uses color instinctively. He has no doubts about what to put on the canvas, and the result is amazing.

OPPOSITE BOTTOM:
Big Red Orange Fantasy Horse, 2007. Oil on canvas, 70 × 84 inches.

I did a different kind of hoof. I did a more powerful rear leg. I did details of Pink Clouds, Blue-White Snow-Capped Mountains. The Hills are Green. The Land has Different Greens. I did details of hooves, lips, mane, ears, tail, and eye with eyelashes.

CHAPTER 2

Facts, Fantasy, Myths, and Reality

"Autism is a complex neurobiological disorder that typically lasts throughout a person's lifetime. It is part of a group of disorders known as autism spectrum disorders (ASD). Today, 1 in 150 individuals is diagnosed with autism, making it more common than pediatric cancer, diabetes, and AIDS combined. It occurs in all racial, ethnic, and social groups and is four times more likely to strike boys than girls. Autism impairs a person's ability to communicate and relate to others. It is also associated with rigid routines and repetitive behaviors, such as obsessively arranging objects or following very specific routines. Symptoms can range from very mild to quite severe."

—www.autismspeaks.org

What is autism? Of course, I know the textbook definition. I cannot begin to keep up with the research, which is compelling and intriguing. But after all these years with Seth, I'm still not always completely clear on what autism is. We know it is not the same for everyone who has it. I have heard some interesting speculations about what autism really is or what causes it. Although I wouldn't bet the farm on any of these theories, perhaps they touch on something real. One of the most far-out theories I have heard is that autistic people represent a new level of evolution. I know it sounds a little strange, but evolution is ongoing so who's to say that humans might not evolve into more sensitive, spiritual beings? Autistic people do have an increased sensitivity to sound, touch, and other people's emotions. Maybe they represent a midpoint of evolutionary change and they do not yet have the bodies to support these changes.

OPPOSITE: *Pink Fantasy Pegasus #1 in Sky Over Land*, 2007. Oil on canvas, 48 × 36 inches.

Fantasy Pegasus is flying over the Lake. The Pegasus has multicolored tail and wings. The Ground is different greens. The Sky is blue with clouds of 3 blues. The Lake reflects the Horse. The Horse is excited. The Background has Lake, Land, & Sky. I feel glad about This Painting. The Mane is light blue and dark blue.

I'm also not completely convinced that autism is solely a problem. It could be a gift. It could be a constellation of sensitivities and abilities that we cannot begin to comprehend. What if there is a generation of autistic people who lack the skills and virtues we reflexively value and who have talents and sensitivities beyond our understanding? What if we are seeing the imperfect vanguard of a new way of being? What if they are the beginning of a kinder, more spiritual, more empathic reality? What if there is a new population of people who cannot go to war, cannot compete, cannot lie, and cannot be unkind? What if they cannot "work" but they can create art? What if they have special talents but lack some of the characteristics by which we define ourselves as humans?

Indulge me for a minute while I linger on the speculative. Do I really believe that we are in the midst of evolution rather than at the pinnacle of evolution? I know that Seth is different. He is "other." Perhaps he has more in common with the mythical creatures he paints than with ordinary humans. He is of this world and at the same time not completely a part of it. Yet, for every thing he can't do that I can, there is something he can do that I can't. He can't cross the street safely. Yet he always knows which way is north. He will never be able to drive. But if he is in a car he can tell you when and where to turn. His spatial orientation is superb. When Seth was eight, he could play Nintendo while holding the controls behind his back. That did not slow him down.

What if he is oriented to altitude, longitude, latitude, temperature, and humidity in ways that we are not? Seth's auditory ability is amazing. He can name any chord or any four random notes struck together for an instant on a piano. Franklin Cohen, principal clarinetist with the Cleveland Orchestra, was amazed when he saw Seth do this. Joe, a composition major at the Cleveland Institute of Music who had won national competitions, laughed with joy when he understood the level of Seth's musical ability. One day Joe said, "Seth tells me what key

Hindemith [a German composer] is in. I never knew Hindemith was in a key." What does Seth hear? How does Seth hear?

When I asked Seth the color of the sea in Grand Cayman, he said, "Purple, indigo, navy, teal, turquoise, and sage." Okay. But when he named the colors as I was staring out at the water, suddenly I could see all of those various hues dancing in the waves. Does he see differently? What if he takes in what we lack the sensitivity to pick up, and what if he lacks the ability to filter out what we reflexively ignore? Do I know for sure? Of course not. I know only that he does not perceive or interact with the world in the same way that I do or that many others do. Because he doesn't speak much, I do not know what Seth knows. He may have abilities that are not yet recognized or understood, let alone acknowledged or admired. He may have gifts and problems we miss because of our assumptions of what we all can do. For example, Seth has no ability to lie. (A gift.) On

The 2 Cayman Groupers, 2008. Oil on canvas, 48 × 48 inches.

The 2 Groupers have Different Hues of Creams, Yellow Ochres, Purples, Light Violets, Sages, Greens, Light Greens, Dark Greens, Blue Greens, Magentas, Maroons, and Pinks. My Friend Diana Schmitt took a photo of this Grouper. My friend Peter Hillenbrand sent me that photo. I added a 2nd Grouper, Coral and Bubbles. The Fish feel calm and comfort. I love the 2 Cayman Groupers.

the other hand, he has no ability to make or keep a promise. (A problem.) It took me twenty-five years to figure that one out! I can tell him not to eat wheat or dairy, to which he is intolerant. He will agree not to, but unmonitored, in a room with cheese and crackers, my gluten-free, dairy-free son would last thirty seconds. At best.

Lately, I am more comfortable with the idea of autism. I fought the label for decades. Maybe it became okay on November 16, 2006, when the *Today* show came to our home. Bob Dotson, Amanda Marshall, and three video and sound people filmed for sixteen hours. Seth was in ecstasy. Karen Sandstrom, a reporter for the *Plain Dealer*, followed with a story on the front page of the Sunday paper on January 28, 2007. She was here for most of January, during the entire painting of *Big Red Orange Fantasy Horse*, coming in and out with photographers, video people, and her daughters. Seth loved every minute of it. Before that, I felt despair. On the one hand was my perfect son whom I adored. On the other was the way the world perceived and discounted him. The dichotomy was unbearable. When he was recognized for his art on a national TV show, I felt that the label didn't mean as much anymore. He was an artist first and autistic second. I never thought anyone else would be as interested in Seth or his world as I was. But now I think there are people who want to learn about him, enjoy his art, and enjoy him.

And Seth is going into the world. In February 2007, I took him to Costa Rica. We went with Ann Kocks and her family. Ann is a family friend who came into our lives when Seth was nine years old. Seth and I became closer and closer with Ann (whom we now see almost every day) until one day Seth said, "Seth has two moms."

We always travel with at least one extra person to help. I always hope Ann can join us and she usually does.

Seth's art exploded with the colors of the tropics. As soon as we got back home, he said, "Galapagos." I saw the paintings that poured out of him and booked Galapagos. We went in November 2007, met with a gallery owner, came home, and four days later we were invited back for our first international opening, in March 2008. In January 2008, Seth said, "Cayman." We went for six days and met with Natalie Coleman, the curator of the National Gallery of the Cayman Islands, who fell in love with Seth and his art. We opened in Galapagos in March and flew home. Seth's art was then in the United Nations for World Autism Awareness Day, and in April we were invited to have a four-month solo exhibition in Cayman, starting October 2008.

My father had loyal friends who started to help us with Seth. Francis Greenburger was like a son to my dad. Now he is always there when I need help and has forged a personal relationship with Seth. Francis is a very busy man but he always finds time to respond to Seth's e-mails. His replies are thoughtful, personal, and chatty. He is a New Yorker, a national and international real estate lion, a major philanthropist, and a supporter of the arts. Francis purchased *Double Lavender and Teal Fantasy Horses*, putting Seth, for the first time, in a curated private collection. In the summer of 2007 he invited Seth to apply for the Art Omi International Artists Residency in Ghent, New York, a three-week program several hours north of Manhattan. Two months later Seth was accepted. In July 2008, Nicollette Ramirez reviewed Art Omi for *Whitehot Magazine* and named Seth as one of the three outstanding American artists of that year's residency. In June 2009, Francis invited Seth to exhibit in the lobby of Time Equities, Inc. at 55 Fifth Avenue in New York City. Seth started a project that would occupy him for the next fifteen months. *Manhattan Floating* is 11 by 26 feet (see page 188–189). It is 104 panels. It is pure Seth. The buildings have wings, and roller coasters wind through the city. The East River has mythic creatures, sea turtles, dolphins, octopi, and coral reefs. The sky has mythic creatures, flying fish, and amusement park rides. Francis opens doors and Seth steps through them.

Perry Finkelman is my father's relative. He, too, is a major player in New York real estate, philanthropy, and the arts. In the summer of 2007 he introduced us to Kip Jacobs, an artist who had provided art and design for Perry's buildings. It was a match made in heaven. Kip is quirky, kind, gentle, and generous. He totally gets Seth. For a week each month in June, August, and December 2007, Seth went to paint in Kip's

Seth Chwast

02-2007

studio. The *Today* show filmed Kip and Seth that December. Kip was Seth's mentor in the Art Omi residency. Seth flew to New York to start working on *Manhattan Floating* in June 2009 and returned in September. He began working on this painting with his artist mentors in Cleveland and Kip in Brooklyn. Kip is working with other developers who may want Seth's art in their lobbies. Seth's dreams are coming true. He is painting in Brooklyn and his art will live in New York. Facts, fantasy, myths, and realities. Who would ever have guessed this would be our story?

MY COMFORT WITH AUTISM HAS unfolded after a long journey. I have accepted the label of autism because it no longer terrifies me. I have come to see that autism didn't stop Seth. More important, I believe Seth will be loved, valued, cherished, and protected by the world, not just by me. As far as autism is concerned, I am no longer certain that autism is a closed book. In 1987, I was told that all changes, all improvements in speech and social contact, would end by age twelve. Now we know that the brain is plastic even for adults; it isn't easily malleable but it isn't set in stone either. I see Seth changing and evolving. Slowly. Steadily. I am not saying that for one second he could pass for normal or take care of himself. However, I don't believe he has hit a ceiling. Not even close.

And how are we, the stewards of the autistic, doing? When Seth was a teenager, a soon-to-be senile, nationally prominent psychologist said, "You've tried everything else to get him to speak. Why don't you try punishment?" If one question could make the universe weep, that one would be a contender. A decade later, it continues to resonate inside me. Because that impulse exists in the world, I feel horror, pain, fear, and sorrow for all the autistic children and their families and for everyone who cannot defend themselves.

OPPOSITE: *Double Lavender and Teal Fantasy Horses*, 2007. Acrylic on wood, 24 × 24 inches.

A) The Background has 2 colors. Teal is over Lavender. The Lavender Fantasy Horse is in Teal Background. The Teal Fantasy Horse is in Lavender Background. The 2 Horses are excited and proud. They are facing each other. The Teal Fantasy Horse has Mane and Tail are Parchment Green Color. The Lavender Fantasy Horse has Blue Spots. The Hooves are Lavender. The Lavender Fantasy Horse has Mane and Tail are Many Different Lavenders. I feel surprised and thrilled. I am glad. The Texture is smooth.
B) The Lavender Horse is on a Teal Background above The Teal Horse is on Lavender Background. The 2 Horses feel Proud and Surprised. The Horses are facing each other. The Teal Horse has Sap Green Mane and Tail. The Lavender Horse has Blue Spot on Horse's Body. I feel Thrilled and Astonished.

I think my attitude about autism and Seth changed because I was willing to go into Seth's world and share his sense of time, his perceptions, and his passions. I just had to get used to a new and different reality. Above all, every day I meet Seth with love. It is my greatest pleasure to do this. There is no way, as I have said, to get Seth to keep a promise. There is no way to get Seth to participate in certain parts of our lives that we perceive as basic. There is no way to get Seth to follow our concept of time. I cannot tell him to take a ten-minute bath and believe it will happen. I cannot threaten, beg, plead, cajole, or shame him into doing what he cannot do. Why would I?

Because we live in the real world, I have to be the bridge between Seth and reality. Sometimes I can say, "We have all day. Take a long, long bath. Come out whenever you want." Most days I have to get him in and out within an hour, which is a challenge. Some days I have to get him out in twenty minutes, which is close to impossible. I move him along by singing. We sing "Come on baby, do the locomotion." Then we switch to "Go [sic] little glow worm, glimmer, glimmer." We do my grade school cheer, "Let's go, let's go, let's really go." I sing a line and point to him and he grins or squeals and sings the next line. His eyes shine. He picks the next song. The bath may still take sixty minutes but it's not two hours. We have fun. Why spend an hour yelling and being angry and punishing him? I am writing these words after Seth has finished a bath. If I were to die and this were my last morning on earth, why leave after an hour of struggle that I was doomed to lose? Instead, I would leave after an hour of singing, joy, and fun. Seth is clean. The job is done. And now he is happily painting. Did I need the time to work on a project or read the paper? Maybe I did, but those things will get done eventually. I cherish my mornings with Seth. They are a privilege, an honor, and a pleasure.

I find it puzzling that so many people support Seth and his journey. It doesn't really make sense. Why are they so excited? Why are they so helpful? It may be that he resonates with people in different ways. Seth is not simply an artist. If he were that, only people in the art world might be excited about him or his paintings. The people who support Seth include people for whom the art world is not very relevant. I think Seth touches people through art, but he also touches something else in people. I think he will reach way beyond the art world. He may become an icon for the autistic, or for everyone who is ignored and dismissed and then, unexpectedly, bursts forth with gifted brilliance. He may be an icon for everyone who is misunderstood, invisible, mocked, or different and then finds a place in the world.

I feel that Seth is becoming safe in the larger world. In addition to me, he has his dad who adores him and takes him to national parks, roller coasters, haunted houses, and the symphony. He has Ann Kocks and her family, whom he loves. He has all his Cleveland artist mentors. He has his zany, free-thinking, tenderhearted, talented Brooklyn mentor, Kip Jacobs. I no longer wonder if anyone will ever appreciate or "get" Seth. The inside circle is growing. As he becomes more visible and as the world gets to see, experience, and enjoy him, concentric circles of interest and affection keep expanding.

Recently we got an e-mail from someone whose name I did not recognize. "Who is it?" I asked Seth. "Amusement park, Ecuador, girl sold tickets." Seth asks lots of people for their e-mail. Americans usually ignore him. But in South America, women working in shops will sometimes give him their e-mail if he asks. When we get home we write. Usually they don't write back. I have Seth take it as far as we can, as he looks for friends. We sent the images of Seth's Galapagos paintings to every address we had in Ecuador. We finally heard back from someone—a heartfelt response received from a young woman, Silvia, who wrote, "I love your pictures. 'Specially because [they] belong to my country, they're great." Seth touches people's hearts.

2 Blue Footed Boobies Standing on a Rock, 2008. Oil on canvas, 24 × 18 inches.

The Birds have Many Different Hues of Creams, Browns, Oranges, Coffees, Peaches, Whites, Peanut Butters, Peanut Shells, Terra Rosa Hues, Rusty Oranges, Tans, Blues, Greens, Yellows, Teals, Turquoises, and Blacks. The Rock has Different Hues of Shiny Colors, Browns, Reds, Creams, Peaches, Oranges, and Grays. The Birds feel happy. I feel glad and enthusiastic. You feel excited. I like Blue-footed boobies. I love Galapagos.

Historically, I have been a shy person, slow to make friends, slow to reveal my essence. Seth is my polar opposite. I love specific people; he loves humanity. I can spend hours alone, daydreaming, thinking about people, crying for people, worrying about people who have no idea they are even on my radar; Seth runs up to people, all people, and asks for their e-mail. He will start a relationship with anybody. I am internal, quiet, spiritual, and private. I do not expect to be seen. I do not have a vocabulary for my thoughts or my spiritual journeys. If I meet someone and they want to talk about the meaning of their life, moments when their reality shifted, or finding internal peace, I am riveted. If I must engage in cocktail party conversations or casual banter I struggle and feel like a fish out of water. Along comes Seth. He will speak to anybody, and one minute later I'm in that conversation. Because his language is limited he needs me to jump in. He wants to make contact so my natural reticence must be overcome so that I can help him. There is no way to quiet or suppress Seth and I see no reason to do so. It's my job to transform and rise to the occasion.

Seth, who has so little language, is the essence of communication. If you exist, he wants to meet you. He wants to know who you are. And he will remember. He wants to know the names of your children, your favorite trips, new buildings in your city. If you tell him where you live, he will go to the computer, look it up, explore the sites and highlights, and take it all in. Seth talks to anyone: women, businessmen, teenagers, men, old, young, people of any size, shape, or color. Everybody counts. Seth is teaching me how to love on the ground, how to reach out, how to meet people wherever they are.

How did autism affect our family? Not always in the ways you might think. It was gut-wrenchingly tough and yet it made my son and me closer than close. We can't have long, meaningful conversations, or communicate in any traditional way. But that does not matter because we can communicate in different ways. We sing, we laugh, and we hold hands. When Seth was diagnosed I never imagined that we would be so deeply connected. The experts said Seth could not connect; they were wrong. (I'm so glad they were wrong!) Having Seth in my life has transformed both of us—time and time again.

The sad truth about families with children with disabilities is that many marriages do not survive. I know I stayed in mine for longer than I maybe should have, in part because Seth adores his dad. We had a difficult marriage and in an odd way, because of Seth's devotion to his dad, autism prolonged it. No matter the circumstances, we had a difficult divorce. I can't speak for Seth's dad or his family so I can't give any specifics about how autism affected them. What I can say is that at the beginning, Seth's dad and I were a team. We worked together for many years to help Seth the best we could. But, as some couples do, he and I diverged more and more, and after thirty-four years of marriage we divorced. I cannot represent here his thoughts, his feelings, or even the full story of our marriage. Was our marriage a casualty of having autism in the family? I will never know for sure. While Seth's father and I no longer work together to help Seth, he and his dad have their connection and activities that enrich Seth's life, and for that I am grateful.

Autism reaches well beyond the immediate family. Some members of our family who live on the East Coast have ever only spent a few days with us and Seth. Was it the autism? Were we too burdened and preoccupied to reach out? Was it the reality of distance? I will never know. My parents were certainly caught up in the maelstrom created by the diagnosis and our quest to help Seth. My mom, Sandra Louise Hilda Newmark, and I had always been close and maintained our connection as I moved away from my childhood home into adulthood and marriage and became a mother myself. She flew to Ohio from New York for Seth's birth and instantly became an adoring and loving grandmother to her new grandson. When the world crashed down on us with Seth's diagnosis, my mom was there to support us and become a lifeline for me. I would put Seth to bed about 9:00 p.m. and he would sing and hum until about 11:00. As I lay next to him in the dark, most nights I called my mother. She kept me company and listened to my pain, my hopes, and my dreams. From the time Seth was diagnosed, until she died, too soon, in a car crash in 1991, we had a six-year connection that buoyed me through a sea of tears and helped me hang on and be the mother that Seth needed me to be.

My father, Milton J. Newmark, loved us. He was fiercely loyal and protective. Autism gave him a challenging task, but nothing could stop him in his defense of his grandson and his search for ways that he could help us. The autism turned him into a lion. If anyone was dismissive of Seth, they were no longer a part of my father's life. Period. If people protected and cared about Seth, they became part of my father's extended family.

In 1999, my beloved father moved in with us and stayed for the last six years of his life. Although Seth had his own room, he decided to be Poppy's roommate. They slept in the same room, ate their meals together, and spent their evenings watching videos or classic movies. My dad loved having Seth keep him company and watched whatever Seth wanted to watch. There was one month when Seth wanted to see *The Yellow Submarine* every night. Then Seth wanted to see different productions of Wagner's the Ring cycle. That continued for two to six hours a night for six months. My dad went along with the video choices willingly and had a good time. They enjoyed a series on magic and another on the sea. Seth and his grandfather totally indulged each other. Whatever one wanted, the other agreed to. They loved being together; they loved each other.

My dad and Seth sat next to each other, sometimes holding hands. I would say, "Seth, heal Poppy. Make Poppy young." Seth would put his hands on my father's head and count backward, starting at age ninety. He'd say, "Ninety, eighty-nine, eighty-eight," and so forth, and my dad would glow with joy. So much for autism and the inability to attach to others. (After we lost my dad, Seth rarely watched TV or videos.)

Seth and my dad had six years of living together. For the first four and a half years, time with my dad was a major part of Seth's life. During the time Dad lived with us, in the middle of the fifth year, Seth discovered

SETH CHWAST   12-19-04

RIGHT: *Self Study #1*, 2004. Charcoal, acrylic, and graphite on canvas, 62 × 52 inches.

Seth. I am happy. Tones of Grays. Seth has a single chin. I am an artist hair. The Self-Study has neck. Emotions. Shades of Gray. Values 1 to 10. Colors on Color Wheel. Dark on left side. Light on right side. The White is in the background. I used acrylic. Opposite of oil is acrylic. The eyes over the ears, nose, mouth, and cheeks. Eyebrows over the eyes. Seth Chwast is taller than Self-Study #1. The Self-Study feels glad. Seth feels astonished and excited by this painting.

painting, and together they were able to celebrate Seth's art. My dad lived to see *Self-Study #1*, Seth's first major portrait. We cherished every painting and every day. Even at ninety, my dad looked to the future. He dreamed of wind power and spoke to Seth about it. I wish he had lived to see Seth's wind power paintings. His dreams will live forever through Seth's art. We lost my dad in October 2005. Two years later Seth was on the Today show, and two days after that he sold *Flower in Red Vase* for $2,200—and was soon painting even more. The slow, leisurely days and nights with my dad occurred when it was perfect for all of us. That time ended, and we soon stepped into a whirlwind of art, beauty, creativity, travel, and the nonstop details of bringing Seth into the world.

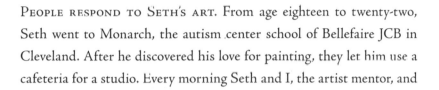

PEOPLE RESPOND TO SETH'S ART. From age eighteen to twenty-two, Seth went to Monarch, the autism center school of Bellefaire JCB in Cleveland. After he discovered his love for painting, they let him use a cafeteria for a studio. Every morning Seth and I, the artist mentor, and

Seth Chwast

09-07-2008

LEFT: *Windmills for Electric Power #1*, 2008. Oil on canvas, 48 × 48 inches.

The Windmills make electric power. I took the canvas outside. I put the canvas on the grass. I painted The Wind in Violet paint. I made 3 Windmills. The Windmills are beautiful. The Grass is Different Hues of Green. The Windmills are Different tones of Grays, White and Black. The Sky is the Wind. The Sky is White and Violet. I feel calm. I feel happy and excited about this painting.

RIGHT: *Flower in Red Vase*,
2003. Oil on canvas,
36 × 18 inches.

Christa, the language therapist, would meet there. Within days Seth had groupies. The computer department came daily. Teachers came. The maintenance people came. One maintenance man explained that he had a brother in South Carolina who couldn't speak but could whittle. This man loved Seth's paintings of hands. He felt Seth was reaching out to his brother, encouraging his brother and blessing his brother. A cafeteria worker told me never to worry about Seth because he was blessed and his paintings made her want to come to work. Another maintenance man told me that every night he went home and told his wife what Seth had painted that day. Seth painting in the cafeteria was a stop for any tour or visitor who came to the building. Seth is a mirror. People look at his art and see something that specifically fills them with peace and joy. Seth had a different mentor and a different theme for each day of the week. Out poured blue whales, fish, hands, auroras, and trees.

People also talk about Seth's art and symbols for communication, freedom, confidence, and growth. In 2005, Dr. Steven Wexberg, a general pediatrician with special interest in children with developmental disabilities, noticed that Seth's earliest paintings (like *Flower in Red Vase*) had a demarcation and change in style between the lower third, which

BELOW: *School of Fish*, 2005. Acrylic on canvas, 24 × 72 inches.

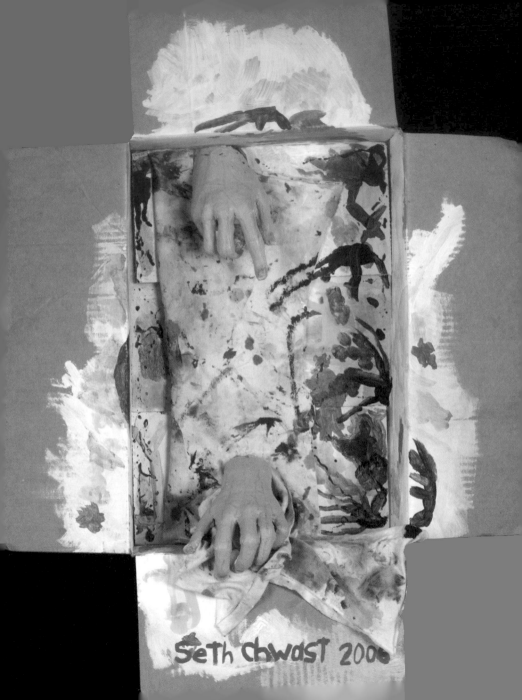

Seth Chwast 2006

OPPOSITE: *2 Hands in the Box*, 2005. Plaster, rag and acrylic on cardboard, 33 × 26 × 8 inches.

ABOVE: *Hand Holding the Pencil*, 2005. Acrylic on canvas, 30 × 20 inches.

LEFT: *Shadow Hands— Warm to Cool*, 2005. Acrylic on canvas, 40 × 30 inches.

was contained and monochromatic, and the upper two thirds, which were more wild, expressive, and colorful. He felt it was a symbol of Seth's breaking out of a constricted world into a freer, more beautiful world, a world with no limits. When Seth made his first horse with a head facing the viewer, a friend said, "Seth is now ready to look the world in the eye." She was right. Seth was going through a sea of change and it showed up first in his art. Don't we all want to burst into freedom, expansion, and color? Don't we all want to greet the world? What a life it would be if everyone could look the world in the eye and say "I'm here" with confidence and excitement, expecting only good things.

When he paints, Seth burns hot and fast, all the while humming and relaxing, smiling and looking like it's a day at the beach. It is so natural and so easy for him. I really didn't understand how good he is. He burns, and I am the one to feed the fire. I am beginning to understand the magnitude of his fire. I stoke it two to eight hours a day. During that time, I schedule mentors, organize exhibitions, write about him, archive his work, and physically deal with over 550 paintings. I believe that I came to earth to do service. I love doing service for Seth. I am the most happy that I have ever been.

Seth wants to change the world. He says, "Seth's art will make people feel all better." I am starting to understand that somehow Seth is a visionary, he is idealistic and loves humanity and symbols and can speak to the world in ways I cannot express, but am starting to witness.

When I tell Seth that he will be famous, he gives his most special smile. He crows with joy. His eyes shine. He is thrilled with every fiber of his being. To Seth, famous means "make people happy."

I do not think Seth is simply the poster man or the poster artist for the autistic. The autism was not vanquished and he did not transform. Whatever it is about him that caused people to dismiss him is still there. The art was probably always there, dormant, waiting for twenty years to be revealed. This time of waiting and incubation may be true for your own child's gifts or your gifts or my gifts. Seth's victory is our victory. It is never too late. The problem becomes the gift. Seth's in-your-face, unmistakable autism is recognized by the moms of the autistic in thirty seconds. They see the autism, and then they see the art, and their hopes for their children change. This possibility of art bursting forth from a child labeled as autistic might bring hope to the world. It might start with the moms of the autistic and spread out to the parents of struggling students, families with a sick child, people with aging parents, those wrestling with every kind of pain. Seth went to Galapagos and made Spanish moms cry with joy. He crossed the equator and changed lives. In the words of Jimmy Durante, I am finally ready to say, "You ain't seen nothin' yet!"

After decades of isolation and darkness, we have walked into the light. All the veils are becoming thin—the veil between the living and the not living; the veils between past, present, and future; the veil between the normal and the differently abled. As we regularly travel to New York, where I grew up, my parents are somehow back in our lives. They are almost as present now as they ever were. My father's legacy lives on in the help we receive from Francis, and in the kindness of Perry, who linked us to Kip. And, anytime we take a trip, I think of my mother, who adored traveling and simply loved fun! Past, present, and future are merging. In my heart, Seth is simultaneously the sweetest baby and the most wonderful man. I can already see him a year from now plowing through his wish list. The heart lives in a different world. I grew up in a world of the mind and suffered mightily. As I move into my heart, I am tapping into a place beyond time and space, beyond logic, beyond fear, beyond doubt and anxiety. I am moving from waking up every day and waiting for the next horrible blow to waking up every day and waiting for the miracles. I feel miracles pour down like rain. I feel that every moment of every day is a blessing. And I hope that this blessing spreads to every single person who wants to open their heart and step into wonder, peace, and bliss. Come with me as we thumb our noses at reality and charge into the world screaming, "No limits!"

Sometimes there is a breakthrough for autistic people. For one moment they make eye contact or come out with a new word or play a game with you. And it's so perfect, so much what you've hoped for, that you wonder how they can go back into their autism. Why don't they stay in our world? I believe that is how we are with the spiritual. We have transcendent experiences, peak moments, or a sense of oneness with the universe. Then we go back to being angry, fearful, ruthless, or self-centered. Once we have made contact with the sacred, why don't we stay? Sometimes I think the autistic have a more constant access to the sacred. I know Seth helped me on my spiritual journey. I think he showed me how to live a full life.

I AM EVER MINDFUL OF SPIRIT, but Seth's physical needs (and my own) require nurture and attendance. Seth's food challenges have consumed us for years. In March 2006, our dear friend Carin Cunningham asked if Seth could do the cover for her book, *Pediatric Gastrointestinal Disorders*. The book was to come out impossibly soon. Could the cover somehow look like Seth's *Fantasy Light Triptych*? I wasn't sure if it was possible. How could anyone make a painting of the digestive tract that came close to the wild colors and fanciful shapes of Seth's paintings of the Northern Lights? I never let Seth hear that request. It seemed too daunting. Every morning, Carin brought over diagrams of the GI system. Every day, Seth did an oil painting. Every night Carin returned to see. Could he do one with the outline of a person? Yes, he could. Could he do one without the outline of a person? Yes, there was *Fantasy Intestines #3*. And somehow the cherry red stomach indeed did

OPPOSITE: *Fantasy Light Triptych*, 2005. Oil on canvas, 40 × 30 inches each panel.

LEFT: *Fantasy Intestines #3*, 2006. Oil on canvas, 20 × 16 inches.

look like *Fantasy Light Triptych*. Four paintings later, there it was. Seth created the painting that was on his first book cover.

Food has been and is a challenge at best, a torment at worst. In 1999, when Seth was sixteen, we went to see Virginia Shapiro, DC, chiropractor and functional medical practitioner in Duluth, Minnesota. We learned that Seth could not tolerate wheat or dairy. This knocked out all his favorite foods and pretty much his entire diet: grilled cheese sandwiches, cheese ravioli, spaghetti with parmesan cheese, garlic bread with melted mozzarella, cheeseburgers, bagels and cream cheese, macaroni and cheese, waffles and cream cheese, blintzes. In a year, Seth, who at 5 feet 11 inches had been slightly overweight, lost thirty-five pounds, going from 205 to 170. He was better able to focus. Sometimes it was difficult to control Seth's diet. Errors were made; there was confusion over what was permitted and what was not. Seth loves most of the forbidden foods and cannot say no to them if they are available. We also heard from those who felt that the diet was nonsense, not scientifically proven and pointless. From their perspective, eating out, good times, and fun were more important than theories.

Thomas Taxman, MD, is a smart, gentle, compassionate pediatric GI doctor with a subspecialty of autism, who is moving increasingly into practicing functional medicine. He is an angel. He works with Seth and me although we are aged out of his primary practice. In April 2009, Dr. Taxman told us about a food sensitivity blood test that measures how your immune cells react to 150 foods and additives. We already knew that Seth has food intolerances (but not allergies) to gluten and dairy. The blood test identifies foods that trigger immune system reactions such as inflammation, headaches, brain fatigue, diarrhea, heartburn, water retention, weight gain, or food cravings. We received information about which foods are safe; which are moderately reactive, and can be enjoyed once every three days; and which are reactive and never to be eaten. We found out that Seth is reactive to and should never have grapes (raisins, wine vinegar, baking powder), honey, pineapple, shrimp, tuna, yeast mix (baked goods, breads, mushrooms, cheese, dried fruit, vinegar, ketchup), baking soda, and yellow squash. There go all the breads, even the ones without yeast. There goes the ketchup. Seth used to eat hamburgers and French fries almost daily, primarily as an excuse to eat ketchup. (He went through a bottle of ketchup a week.) For ten years we gave Seth gluten-free bread, not knowing he was also reactive to yeast, and all the gluten-free, yeast-free products made with baking powder or baking soda. Every morning he had had a pineapple smoothie. We had used honey instead of sugar. Then we found out that sugar is fine and honey is not.

After we started the new diet, Seth went from seven to ten explosive bowel movements a day with blood to two solid bowel movements a day without blood. Now I search for recipes for chicken, turkey, beef, amaranth, quinoa, corn, yams, potatoes, string beans, beets, broccoli, berries, melon, grapefruit, and pomegranate. Of course, there are all the things Seth can eat and won't eat—fish, lamb, veal, duck, and crab. So we find more ways to cook what he will eat. Soon, Seth had a new list of favorite foods that he both tolerated and adored: cashew butter cookies, orange juice, corn chips, hummus, homemade tater tots, buckwheat tortillas with maple syrup, corn tortillas with cashew butter, and dark chocolate cashew clusters. I work to make sure that he has foods that do not simply give him fuel but that are treats and delights. I want to be sure that he is not met with deprivation at the table.

No matter what his dietary issues are, nothing can stop Seth. Colors burst forth from his paintings. The horses that prance across

Purple Pegasus, Head with Stars (Happy Birthday in 2007), 2007. Oil on canvas, 36 × 60 inches.

The Background with Stars and Mountains. The Pegasus has Purple and Lavender Wings with Glow Green Feathers. The Snow-Capped Mountains have 3 blues. The Sky is peach and pink. The Mane is purple. The Horse is happy. The Stars have orange rings. The Horse is flying in the Air. I finished on my Birthday March 30.

Silver Fantasy Griffin #2 with Grayish Purple and with Golden Legs, 2007. Oil on canvas, 36 × 60 inches.

Griffin is a Half Eagle, Half Lion. Griffon is a Roller Coaster at Busch Gardens Europe that will be built in Summer 2007. I love Roller Coasters. I like to ride Roller Coasters starting in 1994. I like to paint Skies. I like Griffins in the Sky. For his Body, I used many Silvers, I used New Colors for the Clouds.

Fantasy Griffin #3 with Grayish Purple Body and with Orange Clouds, 2007. Oil on canvas, 36 × 60 inches.

Griffin is a Half Eagle, Half Lion. Griffon is a Roller Coaster at Busch Gardens Europe that will be built in Summer 2007. I love Roller Coasters. I like to ride Roller Coasters starting in 1994. I like to paint Skies. I like Griffins in The Sky. I made a Different Griffin with Lion's Feet. I made Luminous Orange and Yellow Clouds. The Sky is Yellow.

his canvases are orange, blue, and red—not what you'd find in a typical stable. When he discovered creatures from mythology, suddenly his horses sprouted wings or fins, and fantasy animals came to populate his work.

Seth started his Pegasus series in January 2007. The Cleveland Institute of Art had its month-long winter break. Seth's dear—and maybe only—friend, David, was close with a Cleveland Institute of Art student and brought her over to meet Seth. Within a week, we had three Cleveland Institute of Art students working with Seth and he picked a topic to paint with each of them: auroras, mythical animals, and blue whales. I don't think we will ever know how he chose those particular topics. Out poured a series of whimsical, friendly, joyful Pegasuses, including *Purple Pegasus Head with Stars* and *2 Fantasy Apricot and Orange Pegasus' with Heads in the Sky with Stars*. And then Seth, who follows possibly every roller coaster website, found that Busch Gardens was planning a new coaster, Griffon

TOP: *Turquoise Fantasy Hippocampus with White Coral Reef*, 2009. Acrylic on canvas, 18 × 24 inches.

Turquoise Fantasy Hippocampus is swimming in the Ocean. The Hippocampus' scales have different hues of Silvers, Golds, Creams, and Teals. The Hippocampus's mane is flowing upwards. The Hippocampus's scales have many of different textures, rough and smooth. Turquoise Fantasy Hippocampus is a male, he lives in the Ocean. Turquoise Fantasy Hippocampus feels Happy. This Coral Reef has many corals. The Big Coral has many oval shapes. The oval shapes on the Big Coral are dark and light Turquoises. Turquoise Fantasy Hippocampus is moving his tail. He is a good swimmer! The Coral Reef is a plant. The Medium coral has many Oval Shapes are light Turquoises. This painting is fun and beautiful! I will swim in the Ocean with Friendly Mythic Creature!

(half-eagle, half-lion). Seth did five oil paintings of griffins, including *Silver Fantasy Griffin #2 with Grayish Purple and with Golden Legs* and *Fantasy Griffin #3 with Grayish Purple Body and with Orange Clouds*. He then went larger, to *Twelve Griffins over the Rain Forest in Costa Rica*, which measured 70 by 84 inches.

Seth left the topic of mythic creatures to go where our travels and offerings of openings took him. He painted icons of Manhattan, Galapagos, Cayman, and Trinidad. Then in February 2009 we heard from Bill Lynerd at the Cleveland Museum of Natural History. Seth was already the artist for their Darwin exhibition from June to October 2009. They have booked *Mythic Creatures* from the American Museum of Natural History in New York City. It would now travel and come to Cleveland in 2012. Bill wanted to know if Seth would like to do a companion art exhibit. *Mythic Creatures* is my all-time favorite natural history exhibition. I brought Seth to New York to see it. It was filled with dragons, griffins, winged horses, unicorns, and hippocampi (half-horse, half-fish). Seth already had a whole series of griffins and winged horses. He loves mythic creatures. We said yes. Soon Seth was painting a series of hippocampi, including *Turquoise Fantasy Hippocampus with White Coral Reef* and *Turquoise Shimmer Fantasy Hippocampus*. Each was wonderful in its own way. Then he returned to Pegasus, sketching *Fantasy Pegasus Flying over the Clouds #1*, and then out came *Silver Pinto Pegasus Flying over Golden Sand and Ocean Waves with Brain Coral*. Next, Seth turned to sculpting Chinese dragons. The mythic creatures poured out. The colors were joyful. As was the artist.

OPPOSITE BOTTOM: *Turquoise Shimmer Fantasy Hippocampus*, 2009. Acrylic on canvas, 18 × 30 inches.

I used many Hues of Turquoises and Silvers on this painting. Turquoise Shimmer Fantasy Hippocampus is walking on the Ocean Floor. The Hippocampus's mane is flowing up! The Hippocampus's Tail is Moving back and forth. The Scales have Different Hues of Silvers and Turquoises. The Coral Reef is a plant that lives in the Ocean. There are Many Tiny Coral in the Background. The Big Coral has many details. I drew many Oval Lines on the Big Coral. The Turquoise Shimmer Fantasy Hippocampus Feels gleeful! I feel talented, enthusiastic and proud about this painting! This Painting feels happy!

DO I WANT A CURE FOR AUTISM? Of course. Everybody wants it. May it come soon. If there is a cure for autism and it will help everyone from

TOP: *Fantasy Hippocampus Sculpture #1 with Watermelon Red Horse's Body and Blue Mane,* 2008. White oven-baked clay with acrylic paint, 9.5 × 9 × 7.

The Horse's Body is Watermelon Red. The Mane is Sky Blue. The Fish Tail has Different Hues of Lemon Yellows, Yellow School Buses, Light Greens, Sky Blues, Dark Green Apples, Ocean Greens and Teal Greens. The Fish Tail has a Fin. The Fin is striped. This is a happy Hippocampus.

BOTTOM: *Blue-Violet Fantasy Hippocampus Sculpture #5 w/ Neptune,* 2009. White oven-baked clay with acrylic paint, 8 × 16 × 9 inches.

The Ocean has Different Hues of Blues, Blue Pansies, Blue Poppies, Blueberries, Blue Plums and Blue Fireworks. The Splashwater from the Ocean is on the Hippocampus and Neptune. Hippocampus is a Half Horse, Half Fish. He is swimming and strong and friendly. Neptune is the sea god. He has a trident and crown and skirt and horn of plenty. The Neptune feels gleeful and excited.

Seth Chwast   05-2009

toddlers to adults, and suddenly the whole autism epidemic is just a bad dream and even our adult children are totally safe, what will we learn that will help us with our other challenges? How can we help the struggling students, the shy, the awkward, the atypical, or the ones who are despised by their peers for their talents or abilities? I think the lesson is: Do not give up. I think Seth's and my situation may be more universal than it seems. We are also talking about anyone in a difficult and lonely place. We are talking about the dance between the cared-for and the caretaker. Maybe this is everyone's story.

My life, without my awareness, became a template for letting the challenge and the problem of the child become the path of spiritual growth for the mom. Or, the child's "illness" becomes the mom's "cure." I have learned that when you take a person who is in a dark place, where there is no hope, and bring them to a state of bliss and maintain them in bliss, it does more for you than for them. I did it for my son, who is still autistic. I did it for my dad the last six years of his life. Hope and light become contagious and ignite.

ABOVE: *White Fantasy Hippocampus with Light Blue Ocean Bubbles*, 2009. Acrylic on canvas, 16 × 24 inches.

I drew White Fantasy Hippocampus with Dark Blue Marker. White Paint means happy, gleeful, excited and proud! Seth and the Hippocampus are excited and proud! The Bubbles are Light Ocean Blue. The Hippocampus's Bubbles are made from movement, swimming, running, and playing! This Painting was fun and fantastic to paint! The Bubbles are different sizes, smooth and round. I feel gleeful about White Fantasy Hippocampus with Light Ocean Blue Bubbles! I used 2 colors on this painting, White and Blue.

Seth Chwast

05-08-2001

CHAPTER 3

Roller Coasters and Other Rides

I did not handle the diagnosis very well at first—I was grief stricken. I would call friends on the phone and just babble. If someone innocently asked, "How are you?" the pain would pour out. I tried to gain control. I would tell myself, *Stop! Just stop! Ask her a question. Ask her about her life. I would. But then I'd lose control again, so I'd get off the phone and call* another friend. In those days, I still hoped that Seth only had aphasia (the inability to understand language), that the therapists would help, that he'd grow out of it, and that his brain would compensate. Hope would bring me up, but reality had a way of catapulting me back to earth.

My grandmother was ninety-four when she saw Seth for the last time (she passed away only a month later). He was two. She asked me, "Why doesn't he talk?" I replied, "Buddy [my uncle, her son] didn't talk until three." She shook her head and said, "No, something is wrong." I knew something was wrong. We had a diagnosis but I couldn't accept it; I was hoping it wasn't serious, or that it wouldn't last. I was hoping it wasn't so obvious that even my grandmother, as ill as she was, could see it. I was wrong. I was careening up and down on a ride that seemed to have no end, and I never wanted to be on in the first place.

Later, Seth, on the other hand, found unbounded joy in real roller coasters. Seth's fascination with roller coasters began with a gentle passion for Disney World at age nine. After we lost my mom in the 1991 auto accident, my dad wintered alone in Lake Worth, Florida, near West Palm Beach. I wanted Seth and my dad to spend as much time together as possible, and Seth loved Disney World, too. We started to go to Florida at Thanksgiving and for spring break. We developed a ritual of three days at Disney World, one day at Universal, one day

OPPOSITE: *The Loch Ness Monster*, 2008. Oil on canvas, 40 × 30 inches.

The Loch Ness Monster has many of colors and different hues of Yellows, Buttercups, Buttered-Popcorns, Corns, Bananas, Lemons, Yellow Squashes, Daffodils, Dandelions. Different hues of Greens, Salad Greens, Green Cake Frostings, Green Apples, Green Pickles, Cucumber Greens, Zucchini, Green Peppers, Green Trees, Green Grass, Green Limes, Green Grapes. "Nessie" also known as Loch Ness Monster. I like Loch Ness Monster.

at Busch Gardens, and the rest of the time with my dad. School and therapy were important. But Seth knowing his grandfather and going to Disney World and playing in the sand were also important.

"In the end," I said, "I prefer Disney to reality." At that time I did. It was a place where Seth was safe, happy, and in control. All his life, Seth has tried to make sense of the world. He has a massive intellect, and there are always systems that intrigue him. Letters and numbers were first. Then came Legos and construction. Then Nintendo. Then roller coasters. Each of these are finite worlds that he can master. But mastering social cues or answering questions such as, "What's new?" are like climbing Everest for Seth. He would be lost in a room with three kids who are talking and interacting.

Disney was a world that Seth could handle. He knew each "land" by heart and he would lead the way. He knew every ride, every restaurant, and every show. Every morning he would pick the land, the restaurant, and plan the order of the rides. Essentially, he could be in control of his universe. Roller coaster facts, Seth's favorite topic, are safe and easy for him. He uses them to have conversations, although they do not do much to break the ice with another person. Most people who are met with a volley of Seth's facts are usually too perplexed to know how to react or respond. Seth had no way to connect with other kids or to be a part of a conversation. So we did language therapy nonstop to crawl inch by inch toward the mountain of speech that any three-year-old could master. But, twice a year, we said "So long" to reality and headed off to Disney World.

From there we branched out. Kyle, his nanny who had been with Seth since he was three, took Seth to Geauga Lake, a local Ohioan amusement part, about thirty minutes away, every week all summer. Then in 1994, when Seth was eleven, Kyle took him to the famed Cedar Point amusement park in Sandusky, Ohio.

Roller Coasters and Other Rides

Seth was determined to go to Cedar Point, but at the same time he was petrified. On the appointed day, Kyle and Seth set off (about a four hours' ride roundtrip) but pulled off the road at every rest stop, where Seth would throw up or have diarrhea. Kyle called me. Should they keep going? Should they come back home? Seth wanted both. They did this the whole morning: drive, stop, call, drive, stop, call. Finally, when they got to Cedar Point, Seth refused to go on the roller coaster and at the same time refused to go home. Kyle called me again. She finally put him, screaming in terror, in the seat next to her for his first coaster ride of the day. He got off laughing and ran to get in line for the next coaster! The following week they went through the whole cycle again. Stop, start. Stay, go. This lasted all summer. The next year he had no fear and would ride anything.

My dad wanted Seth to be safe in a large, heavy car, so he gave us his old Lincoln Continental to be used just for Cedar Point trips. Sometimes they went daily. Kyle and Seth put three thousand miles on that car in one summer, driving back and forth to the amusement park. Those trips also served as an opportunity for Seth to make some friends, or at least have contact with kids his age. Other parents did not want to drive four hours to the amusement park and back and were thrilled to send their kids with Seth and Kyle.

Seth continued to develop coaster rituals. For many years, we went from park to park in Pennsylvania, starting with Conneaut Lake, then Waldameer Park in Erie, Kennywood Park in Pittsburgh, Idlewild Park in Ligonier, Lakemont Park in Altoona, DelGrosso's in Tipton, Knoebels in Elysburg, Williams Grove in Mechanicsburg, Hershey Park in Hershey, and culminating with Dorney Park in Allentown. Seth was determined to see them all. Roller coasters and amusement parks put Seth into a state of ecstasy. We would not have missed any of those trips for the world.

In January 1997, we drove to Chicago for our first trip to the No Coaster Con (Conference). I kid you not. ACE (American Coaster Enthusiasts) holds a yearly conference where there are no coasters to ride, but the roller coaster parks come and do presentations on the coasters under construction that will be open by summer. When we went, the conference was presided over by Marty, a judge in a Hawaiian shirt who had a never-ending collection of jokes. The conference started at 8:00 a.m. and finished at 6:00 p.m. Seth was the first one seated and almost the last to leave. By the end of the conference, he had memorized pretty much every presentation. When his interest is high, nothing can stop him.

Our year developed its own shape, its own rituals. For many families, the year starts in September with the new school year. For us September was the last flurry of roller coaster days, with the last weekend devoted to the beginning of haunted house season. I had zero interest in haunted houses, but Seth loved them, and he was so joyful when he went through them that it was a pleasure to take him. We would drive every Friday, Saturday, and Sunday nights to haunted houses, haunted mazes, or haunted hayrides. His favorites—the haunted laboratory and the haunted schoolhouse—were in Akron. That was always our opener.

November was devoted to Florida—my dad, Disney World, and the beach. Then it was time to plan Christmas. Sometimes we went to Pittsburgh for Christmas to visit friends, came home and had a New Year's party, and then flew to Atlanta. Sometimes we went right from Pittsburgh to Atlanta and did New Year's there. Either way it was wonderful. January was the No Coaster Con. Then it was time to call Disney World and start planning spring break in mid-March. In the cold of late winter, we had big dinner parties with friends. Finally spring would come, and the second Saturday in May was the opening day at Cedar Point. Seth liked to stay near the park the night before and be there when it opened. Then we had roller coasters all summer.

Seth keeps up many of these rituals and now does them with his dad. The year starts again in September with the last glorious days of roller coasters, drives in the country to see the leaves, and the wait for the haunted houses. Not a bad life! It's certainly not what I expected. But he loves it.

Many options were not open to us. We took the opportunities for fun and joy as best we could. We lived them. We loved them. Long conversations, poetry readings, school plays, debate team, and Little League sports were not in the cards for Seth. So we did Disney World, haunted houses, hosted great parties, followed our roller coaster rituals, and enjoyed going to the theater and musicals (we went to every musical that came to Cleveland; Seth loved musicals). For Seth, this was his life. And for me?

Life was like a camera with a zoom lens. When I zoomed in, focusing on Seth and all his interests and talents, all was well. For example, Seth was musically talented. His music therapist was amazing and Seth loved music therapy. There was progress each week. But when I zoomed out

Haunted House, 2008. Oil on canvas, 18 × 24 inches.

The Monsters have different hues of Purples, Strawberries, King's Blue Deeps, Red Roses, Green Leaves, Green Cake Frostings, Green Salads, Pink Cake Frostings, Teals, Turquoises, Yellow Cake Frostings, Peanut Butters, Candy Apple Reds, Oranges, Yellow Bananas, Yellow Lemons, Violets, and Purple Grapes. The Monsters feel excited and happy. The House has walls and roof have shingles. This painting feels happy.

and saw Seth in the external world, it was altogether different. The pain could rip me in half. I struggled to find my balance and keep centered, to cheer him on and keep him happy. I knew I needed to do something for myself. I started to turn to the spiritual like a flower turns to the sun.

I found new friends and went back to old relationships. I started leading dream workshops and studying Kabbalah. My marriage unraveled. While we were a good team for Seth, my husband was uncomfortable with my spirituality. There was nothing I could do to resolve this conflict. The pain of our marriage disintegrating was unbearable. At the same time I was moving into a quiet inner place of peace, joy, and even bliss. The twists and turns of life with Seth seemed to be evening out and I found that when I was able to reach inside of myself, I was much more able to support and care for him.

In the same way that I had been on an emotional roller coaster, I realized that the roller coaster may be a metaphor for Seth's essence. At times, he is languid. The word *hurry* has no meaning for him (especially when it comes to baths). But he can move fast, too. He can paint all day. Presently he is creating about a hundred paintings a year. Some of them—many, actually—are six by seven feet. He once rode seventeen roller coasters in two hours. He is speed and fire and even his mother doesn't know how fast or hot he burns. Maybe the roller coaster talk has a deeper importance to him.

It's no wonder that Seth's two loves—roller coasters and art— would come together; once again, as most things with Seth, it happened in an unexpected way. He checks multiple websites daily to follow all the roller coaster news. In June 2008, just before Seth was to go off to the Berkshires to participate in the Art Omi International Artists

Residency, he read about a seventeen-year-old boy who had lost his hat on Batman: The Ride at Six Flags Over Georgia. The boy had climbed over two six-foot "Do Not Cross This Line" fences, went under the coaster to get his hat, and was decapitated. Seth spoke of this incident daily, if not hourly. He also talked about the girl who lost her feet on Superman Tower of Power at Six Flags Kentucky Kingdom.

The second day of Seth's residency at Omi we were with Kip Jacobs, Seth's mentor. We were discussing the subject of Seth's next painting.

Kip: I have to earn a living. I paint on commission. I have no choice what I paint. You're supporting Seth. Why not let him paint what he wants?

Me: I do. I always do.

Kip: He wants to paint the boy who lost his head. It's the only thing he talks about. Will you let him?

Me: No. [Silence.] What will it do to Seth to focus on it? What will it do to his soul? What will we do with the painting? Who would buy it? Who would put it in their living room?

Kip: It will go into a museum. You have to trust him.

[Silence.]

Me: Give me until tomorrow.

The next morning I said that Seth could paint whatever he wanted. I never dreamed that Seth would want to paint a decapitation. And I

RIGHT: *The Boy Was Decapitated on Batman: The Ride at Six Flags Over Georgia on Saturday, June 28, 2008*, 2008. Acrylic on canvas, 60 × 72 inches.

The boy feels happy. The Boy's head died. The Boy's head goes to Venus. 17-year old boy died. I used different colors of Flesh in Boy's Head. I like drawing of sketch of boy lost his head. Decapitate means cut out. Kip Jacobs is my friend. Kip and Seth painted the Roller Coaster. This is our first Gilbert and George painting. The Boy's Eyes are Blue. I will paint the Girl who lost her feet.

OPPOSITE: *The Girl Who Lost Her Feet*, 2008. Acrylic on canvas, 72 × 30 inches.

In 2007 The Girl rode on *Superman: Tower of Power* at Six Flags Kentucky Kingdom. Cable broke. Girl lost her feet. I wanted to do this painting. I used colors of Pink, Gray, and White of Flower Shirt. This is my first flower shirt.

didn't realize he was asking to do so. I asked Kip: "How did you know?" Kip told me, "I listened to him. It's the only thing he talks about. Just listen. He will tell you what he wants to do. After this, he wants to paint the girl who lost her feet."

Kip gave Seth a sketchpad and told him to draw the boy who lost his head. Out came a little archetypal guy in the lower left-hand corner—no head, no gore—and a large smiling head floating in the sky in the upper right-hand corner. Seth, who is iffy on what death means, said the boy will grow a new head and the head will grow a new boy. As he sketched he was humming and not in the least upset. Together, Kip and Seth went to the computer to look through images of Batman: The Ride. Seth, who knows this coaster intimately, picked the angle he wanted to paint. He walked up to a 60-by-72-inch canvas and proceeded to draw and then

happily paint the headless boy, the cap, and the beautiful large floating head. Seth had recently learned of Gilbert and George, the British artists who work on paintings together. Now, just for this painting, Seth and Kip did the coaster together and labeled it as such. The essence of the painting is the boy, the hat, and the head. Next, Seth was eager to get on to painting the girl who lost her feet. He made a sketch of a sweet, smiling girl and two feet, soles facing the viewer, and then enlarged it onto a 72-by-30-inch canvas.

Although he may not understand death or injury in the same way we do, Seth knew something was wrong and spoke about these tragedies nonstop. After completing the paintings, he never spoke about either incident again. It was as if by creating the paintings, he put the incidents to rest in his own mind.

These works also released a flood of creativity. Earlier, he finished *Firecracker* in June 2006, working with a level to create a fantasy roller coaster. In September 2006 he created more roller coaster studies and cloud studies. Now, humming and smiling, Seth went on to finish *The Coney Island Parachute* and *The Treehouse*. He started a village, a city, a world of cutouts, acrylic on wood. *The New York City with Village People* is the first grouping. But only the first.

The New York City with Village People, 2008. Acrylic on wood cutout, 21 × 62 inches.

The Icons of Village are cutouts of Houses, Clouds, Water Towers, People, Trees, Signs, Cars, and a Fire Hydrant. I used many of colors on Icons. The Village People are happy.

Back home, Seth continued to paint his passions. Soon we had *Haunted House* (see page 59), *The Coney Island Wonder Wheel* (see page 68), and *The Cyclone* (see page 69). Joan Perch, his first agent, came to our house to curate an opening. In the studio, paintings cover every surface, including the floor. She laughed and said she never before curated an exhibition from art lying on the floor.

The art kept pouring out. As Seth started working on *Manhattan Floating*, more rides appeared. *The Ferris Wheel and Pinkus Monster* and *Chelsea Parachute Jump with Flying Fish* filled him with joy.

I had twenty years of pain, confusion, exhaustion, and despair. I hoped for a cure and never got one. I was loyal and determined. I moved heaven and earth to find ways for Seth to be normal. When that didn't work, I moved heaven and earth to give him a great life. At age twenty-eight Seth is still autistic. He is also happy, productive, and usually in a state of ecstasy. He is on the cusp of being recognized for the true artist he is. As a mother, to know the veil of being defined autistic is being lifted to reveal Seth as an artist is my bliss.

Coney Island Parachute Jump, 2008. Acrylic on canvas, 72 × 30 inches.

I started this painting in Brooklyn in June. I finished it at Art Omi. The Parachute Jump has Different Colors. I used Neon of Red, Orange, Green, Magenta, Light Violet, Yellow, Pink, Purple, and Cream. It is a fun painting. I feel excited.

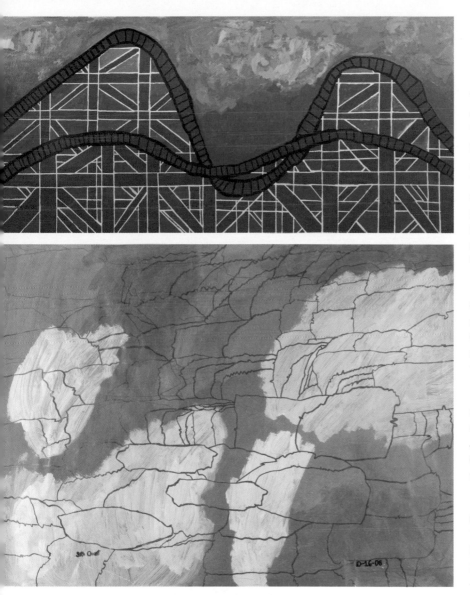

TOP: *Firecracker*, 2005. Acrylic on wood, 40 × 84 inches.

I mixed Blue and White colors to make the sky. The structures are made of wood and have many of diagonals. The track has many of lines, curves, waves, and hills. Wooooaaaa!

CENTER: *Cloud Studies, No. 3*, 2006. Graphite, acrylic wash, and marker on paper, 18 × 24 inches.

BOTTOM LEFT: *Roller Coaster and Cloud Study, No. 4*, 2006. Graphite on paper with marker, 18 × 24 inches.

BOTTOM RIGHT: *The Treehouse*, 2008. Pencil on paper, 24 × 18 inches.

The Trees have windows and doors. The Trees have leaves. The Clouds are in the sky. The Treehouse Building is very tall. It has crooked. The Trees have branches. The Treehouse Building has windows on crooked. I made 14 linocuts of this drawing.

The Coney Island Wonder Wheel, 2009. Oil on canvas, 18 x 24 inches.

I have been to Coney Island in 1998, 2000, 2002, and 2008. The Wonder Wheel is still there. I rode on Wonder Wheel many times. I like swinging in the Wonder Wheel. The Wonder Wheel has Different Hues of Orange Marmalades, Orange Carrots, Orange Clementines, Cantaloupes, Papayas, Mangoes, Macaroni and Cheeses, Nacho Cheeses, American Cheeses, Cheddar Cheeses, Goldfish Cheese Crackers, Cheese Curls, Grilled Cheeses, Cheeseburgers, Marigolds, Orange Fireworks, Orange and Yellow Autumn Leaves, Yellow Bananas, Yellow Fireworks, Yellow Dandelions, Yellow Sunflowers, Yellow Daffodils, Yellow Roses, Cerulean Blues, Cobalt Blues, Blue Cake Frostings, Blueberry Muffins, Blueberry Pies, Blueberry Yogurts, Blue Pansies, Blue Irises, Blue Fireworks, King's Blue Lights, Turquoises, Green Cake Frostings, Green Salad Lettuces, Green Granny Smith Apples, Green Christmas Trees and Green Christmas Wreaths, Green Mint Leaves, Very Very Dark Purples, Purple Grapes, Purple Irises, Purple Crocuses, Purple Hyacinths, Fuchsias, Orchids, Purple Fireworks, Purple Tulips, Pink Grape-fruits, Purple Laser Shows, Magentas, and Maroons.
I like this painting.

Coney Island Cyclone, 2009. Oil on canvas, 40 x 30 inches.

The Cyclone has Different Hues of Yellows, Yellow School Buses, Yellow Lemons, Teals, Turquoises, Greens, Green Cake Frostings, Green Lettuces, Green Salads, Mixed Greens, Pinks, Hot Pinks, Reds, Crimsons, Dark Reds, Red Candy Apples, and Blues. The Sky has Different Hues of Multicolors. *Cyclone* is a Steel Coaster w/ Wooden Track. Cyclone is keeping it. Not tearing down. I rode *The Cyclone* in Summer 1998, Summer 2000, May 2002 and June 2008. I love *The Cyclone*. Goodbye Astroland. Astroland is old name for Amusement Park at Coney Island. I love Coney Island.

FIN ON VENUS

Seth Chwast   05-28-0

CHAPTER 4

"New Friends Are Everywhere"

Seth has a number of phrases that burst forth from him seemingly randomly. I don't know where he acquired them, but they express the essence of who he is. One of the phrases, "New friends are everywhere," is a reminder to me of the wonderful angels who have come into our lives over the years. Each one has become a guide or a bridge for Seth into new experiences and has helped bring him more and more into the world. Or perhaps these angels and helpers have crossed a bridge into Seth's world. No matter, we could not be where we are today without the wonderful families, friends, artists, and others who have connected with Seth over the years. One of our most memorable was a dog.

When Seth was three, I saw an ad for service dogs. The ad explained that the dogs were for quadriplegics, paraplegics, the deaf, and the aphasic—my word for what was going on with Seth (since I still wouldn't use *autistic*). Because I'd never seen services specifically for the aphasic, I would have applied no matter what they were offering. I applied, got pregnant, had our application accepted, bought a home, sold a home, miscarried, and we flew to California for the dog.

These service dogs had received two years and $10,000 worth of training. The agency, Canine Companions for Independence, represented by their head trainer, Mary, had two goals: to match each person with the proper dog and to make sure the new owner knew enough and was committed enough to keep the dog safe. We found ourselves in a large room in Santa Rosa, outside of San Francisco, with twelve paraplegics and quadriplegics, and a woman named Karen Frechette who was getting a dog for her nine-year-old son Joey (he had a genetic disorder and had stopped growing at four, and was not expected to live

OPPOSITE: *Fin on Venus*, 2005. Acrylic on paper, 11 × 8 inches.

The Dog is White. The Dog is a friend. The Dog is a mammal. The Dog is Infinity Chwast. He is Seth's Dog. He is died. He is on Venus. Seth stays on Earth. I feel anxious about Infinity Chwast. I love him a lot. The Venus is a 2nd Planet from The Sun.

very long). This group would be together in "boot camp" for two weeks. (Mary, Karen, and I stayed friends for the next twenty years.)

The first day, Mary talked and then let fourteen dogs race around the room. They were so vital, powerful, and alive—and we, the humans, were so in need of their energy. That night, volunteers brought us pizza for dinner. I sat down, took a slice, and began to eat. The man next to me said, "Selfish, aren't we?" I was startled by his injured tone. Then I realized he was a quadriplegic and couldn't feed himself. So I fed him. It seems we were in need of each other's energy as well.

For two days we worked briefly with each dog. The third day, Mary made the first set of matches. I liked about ten of the dogs and *really* liked six of them. Seth had been with every dog. He ignored all of them except Yreka, a beautiful golden retriever. Seth, who was now four and almost never spoke, said, "Rika." I don't know if Mary knew about Seth liking Yreka and I never thought to tell her. But the day the dogs were given out, one by one, I was thrilled when I heard Mary say, "Seth, you get Yreka." I lunged for Yreka, buried my head in his neck, and cried with relief. He was my all-time favorite. Every morning for the remainder of the training period, some dogs would be switched. Your dog could be perfect for you, but if someone else in the group wasn't doing well with their dog, Mary would make adjustments until everyone had a dog that worked well with them. If you already liked your dog, morning was a time of dread. Until the last day, you could lose your dog. One man lost his five times. This was not easy. In a very short time, your dog became a lifeline that you felt you could cling to. When it was taken away it became yet another loss on whatever journey had brought you to seek a canine companion in the first place. Every morning I feared losing Yreka. But Seth never had to change his dog for another.

After these sessions, we flew home from San Francisco. As we went through security, I was holding Yreka's leash when the inspector asked,

OPPOSTE: *Yreka, Studies*, 2008. Graphite on paper, 12 × 18 inches.

Seth Chwast   Yreka   11-21-08

"Is he going to pee on my rug?" I replied, "Oh no, he's had ten thousand dollars' worth of training. He's a service dog. He would never pee on your rug." The man looked at me and said, "Not the dog. The boy!" Seth was standing there, pants around his ankles, holding his penis. I scooped him up and we ran for a bathroom.

The next year we flew to West Palm Beach to visit my parents. Yreka was never separated from Seth, and he flew on the plane curled up under Seth's feet, wearing his backpack for identification. It was a long flight, and when we landed I knew that Yreka had to pee so I led him to the bushes. I noticed a policeman watching us. When Yreka finished, the policeman walked over (West Palm Beach is not known for liberal policemen). I thought, *This is it.* But then the policeman asked, "Hey, is that the dog I saw on *Oprah?*" I smiled and replied, "No, but he's a service dog," and I went on to tell the policeman everything Yreka can do. He said, "I'm going to tell my wife that I saw that dog."

One of Yreka's jobs was to be a social magnet and attract kids into Seth's life. Boy, was he a success! Everyone adored him. Yreka was also a physical anchor. Seth had a leash with Velcro on the inside of the handle. When we closed the Velcro, boy and dog were attached. If Seth ran, Yreka would run with him. Usually, whenever I called Seth, he stayed absorbed in whatever he was doing and didn't respond. But now I could call Yreka, who would immediately come, bringing Seth with him. If I needed to let go of Seth, I could attach him to Yreka, tell Yreka to sit, and Seth couldn't run off. For the first time since

BELOW: *Yreka Chwast*, 2008. White oven-baked clay with acrylic and copper oil paint, 4.75 × 6.5 × 3 inches.

The Dog's Head has Different Hues of Coppers, Browns, Golds, Creams, Browns, and Whites. Yreka is a mammal. Yreka is my Dog. When I was 4 years old in 1987. Yreka is a Golden Retriever. Yreka is a friendly, happy, and not mean Dog. Yreka from San Francisco to my House. Yreka went to Wendy and Jim's House. Yreka went to the Achievement Center School every day w/Seth. Yreka went to Florida and rode on the Plane w/Seth. Yreka went to New York w/Seth. Yreka went to Trick-or-Treat w/Seth. Yreka went to Movies w/Seth. Yreka went to Lopez y Gonzales Restaurant w/Seth. Yreka pulled Seth in a Wagon. Yreka died in 1998. Yreka feels happy. I feel anxious about Yreka dying. I love Yreka. I miss him.

Seth was diagnosed, I felt safe. For the first time in Seth's life, I had help 24/7. But Yreka's main job was to comfort Seth. He went with Seth to school, to medical appointments, to dental appointments. He was by Seth's side when he had to go into the operating room and have general anesthesia to get a dental cavity filled. (Try to imagine that one!) Yreka was also my comfort through difficult times. He was the Buddha of dogs. When Yreka was too old to work, he became our pet and lived with us for three more wonderful years. We became a two-dog family and Seth got a new canine companion.

Our second service dog was Infinity, referred to by Seth as Fin or Infinity Chwast. He was a silly, goofy, loving, champagne-colored golden retriever who came to us in the fall of 1995. Mary, who knows and loves Seth, wanted him to be Seth's special dog. As we were getting closer to Halloween, the first thing she did was teach Infinity to bob for apples! Seth loved both dogs and was very sad when each dog died. We lost Fin when Seth was twenty-two. He immediately painted *Fin on Venus*. Later he sculpted *Infinity Chwast* and *Yreka Chwast*. Seth thinks everyone who dies goes to live on Venus with Elvis. He could be right.

WE TOOK SETH TO THE CLEVELAND Music School Settlement before age two for an evaluation for music therapy. The director, Louise Steele, did all the evaluations but did not add any new cases to her

ABOVE: *Infinity Chwast*, 2008. White oven-baked clay with acrylic paint, 4.5 × 6 × 3.5 inches.

Infinity's Head and Neck have Different Hues of Whites, Flavored Butter Popcorns, Cream Cheeses, Cream, Cheesecakes, Butters, and Margarines. The Fin's Ears and Eyebrows are Peanut Butters, Creams, Peanut Shells, Cashew Crunches, Coffees, and Peanut Brittles. The Fin's Eyes and Nose are Different Hues of Browns, Hot Fudges, Fudges, Chocolates, Dark Browns, Soils, and Dark Chocolates. Infinity is a Dog's Name. Infinity is my Dog. He is a Golden Retriever. Fin feels happy. I feel proud. I love Infinity. I miss Infinity.

workload. She insisted on being alone with Seth for the evaluation. At that time we never let anyone take Seth without me or his father also being present. She insisted, and said we could watch through a one-way mirror. She was good. She was more than good. When it was over I told her, "Please take him! I'm going to lie on the floor and hold your feet and beg until you agree to take him!" So she did, seeing Seth twice a week for the next sixteen years, stopping only when she moved out of town. I believe she truly loved him. She transferred him to Lori Smith, who is now going on year ten as his music therapist, advocate, and friend.

Christa Hanzmann Stancato was a speech student when she answered an ad I had posted in the Speech Department at Case Western Reserve University when Seth was two. She called and told me, "I've been reading about aphasia all day. Is the job still open?" (We didn't know that the job would be "open" for the next twenty-six years!) She worked with Seth three hours a day twice a week until he was twelve, when she got married. She saw him when she was a college student, when she was getting her master's degree, and when she had become a professional language therapist. At her wedding, she asked Seth to be the ring bearer. I had no idea if he could do it, but she trusted him. In the end, he walked down the aisle in front of two hundred people and brought her the ring. During the reception, he sat next to her on the dais. At that time he ate only SpaghettiOs. In the wedding pictures you can see cans of SpaghettiOs right there on the table, next to the bride's plate. Life was good to us, and when Seth went to Monarch, the autism school of Bellefaire JCB, at age eighteen, they hired Christa as his language therapist. From then on she worked with him two and a half hours a day until he graduated at age twenty-two in June 2005. She is still in his life—an angel!

Denise Montalvo Cerino was studying special education when she came to us and Seth was four. She stayed until Seth was eleven, seeing him twice a week—first when she was a student and then as a certified teacher. She had Seth write his first (and only) book report. He drew a picture of a helicopter and dictated one sentence.

Kyle Corwin became Seth's nanny when he was three. She stayed until he was sixteen, when she left to have her own child. Kyle had great self-esteem and a big mouth and was afraid of no one. This was useful because she, Seth, and the dog were always being taken to the police station for bringing a dog into a public place. Kyle was also a good sport—very friendly and full of fun.

It was recommended that Seth spend as much time as possible with peers who had normal speech. In Cleveland, Ohio, in the 1980s, people had birthday parties for their kids with cake and ice cream. There was one little boy whose mom, for his three-year-old birthday party, provided pony rides for the guests. But that type of party was unusual. I decided to pull out all the stops and for Seth's third birthday I had a petting zoo. Then I'd throw a blow-out party once a month. I'd do practically anything to bring in the kids for Seth to see and (hopefully) interact with. My address book, under P for "Party," had the names of clowns, magicians, balloon ladies, face painters, and so on. One year we had a party that featured a boa constrictor. I used my camera to do portraits of each family with the snake. Those were festive, happy days.

I told my friends that Seth needed to be with kids his age. They were wonderful about coming over and bringing their children. Every Wednesday afternoon Kathy and Cher would come over with their kids. Under Kyle's supervision, all the children would go off to play. We adults would put our feet up and tell stories. Life was good.

My friends Vicky and Sam were able to enter Seth's world and respond in the most generous, kind, and matter-of-fact way as if all was normal, acceptable, and even wonderful. One day we went to their house for dinner and brought over a box of pastries for dessert. After dinner, one of their kids came out and said, "Seth is trying on the dessert." We walked into the kitchen. Seth was streaking a finger through the whipped cream, looking at it, wiping it on his clothing, and then doing the same with the next pastry. He looked like an abstract painting. Everyone smiled. Twenty years later, Vicky and Sam are still willing to listen to my pain and celebrate our victories. Their gentle laughter centers me and dissolves my anxiety when life seems too raw.

We also had friends with children who lived out of town. Emily and Eugene and their two children, Chris and Doyle, who lived in Pittsburgh, became our extended family. Every six weeks or so we'd load up our car with festive foods and drive to their house for the weekend. At Christmas we'd bring a car full of gifts and stay with them for a week. Seth loved to wrap gifts. Every morning we would awaken to the smell of freshly baked bread, courtesy of Eugene. Meals with them were like something out of a Norman Rockwell painting: turkey, homemade cranberry pear sauce, mashed potatoes, fresh rolls, sweet butter, and homemade cakes and pies. We would bring barbecued beef, New York strip steaks, and Christmas cookies baked by Seth and Kyle. Eugene would take Seth into his woodworking shop to build with him. Seth loved to hammer and glue. Eugene let him use the saw and Seth would build little toy boats out of scraps of wood. Chris, who was eleven when Seth was born, still comes to visit.

Our friends Lis and Nick lived in Atlanta with their three children. We went to visit them three times a year. One day as we were standing on their deck talking and Nick was smoking a pipe, Seth (then four

Abstract in Oil with Roller Coaster and Christmas Tree, 2008. Oil on canvas, 24 × 18 inches.

It is a Fantasy Roller Coaster. It is a Fantasy Christmas Tree. I used some thick paint and some thin paint. I used many colors. I feel happy when I look at the painting. I like the Christmas Tree. I feel excited about the Roller Coaster. I like painting and sculpting with paint. I used brush and I squeezed paint on the canvas. I like Roller Coasters and I like Christmas.

years old) came over to Nick, unzipped Nick's fly, and started to put his hand in. I couldn't breathe! But Nick just continued to puff on his pipe, saying, "Here, Seth," as he reached into his pocket and took out the lighter he had used a minute before. "Is this what you're looking for?" he asked. Seth was mesmerized when Nick showed him how to use the lighter. Nick is a pediatric neurologist. He never missed a beat!

In the real world, people stared or started to talk to Seth and were mystified when he didn't answer. There was always an awkward moment of wondering when to say, "He's got a little trouble with language," when to say nothing, and when to leave. With our friends, there was nothing to explain, and I felt comfortable and safe.

Friends were great, but this wasn't enough. I put up signs at three nearby colleges, looking for various kinds of mentors for Seth. We already had two student mentors, Christa and Denise. We needed more. I tried every department: speech, music therapy, special education, and social work. I'd interview students and if I liked them, I'd say, "This is the best job in the world!" And then the students would come and work with Seth and they'd tell me, "This is the best job in the world!" I started hiring students to work with Seth when he was two. I loved Seth; his dad loved him; his nanny loved him. But we got tired. There's nothing like having someone come in once a week for three hours all geared up and ready to go. They'd ask what they should do and I'd say, "Do whatever you want. Follow your passion."

One of the students baked cookies with Seth, having him read the directions, measure, mix, and stir. Jason was an athlete. He took Seth to a program for special needs kids where they would swim and jump on a trampoline. Then they'd go to Jason's apartment and play Scrabble. Nathan came for years. He invited Seth to his high school graduation party, where he, his mom, and their friends played Irish music. The next summer Nathan took Seth, at age twelve, to travel camp. This meant daily visits to museums, amusement parks, and the Amish countryside, culminating in a three-day trip at the end of each of the three-week sessions. Seth was the first special needs child to participate in this program. Nathan grew up and became a physician. Becky, who worked as a stage manager for a summer theater festival, took Seth into the backstage world of theater where he met actors, lighting people, costume designers, and more. She is the one who introduced him to art, taking him to his first art class at the Cleveland Museum of Art, and working on oil paintings with her at her apartment. Once a week Becky invited Seth to spend time with her and her roommates and have an opportunity to be with young people close to his age. This was heaven!

When Seth started to paint in the cafeteria of Monarch, his autism school, for a while, his main mentor, Donna, was not available, so I asked everybody I knew for suggestions for additional artist mentors. By January 2005, I had four artists/angels willing to give it a try. I found them and talked them into it; I paid them. Every morning, we'd meet at Seth's school. It was me, Seth, the artist, and Christa. I promised the artist, "Just try it. You won't have to be alone with him. I will be there. Christa will be there. We will stay for as long as you need us. I want you to be comfortable. I want you to love this." I gave each artist whatever he or she wanted. Oil paints? Fine. Acrylics? Fine. Your own brushes no one else uses? Fine. I paid. I prayed. I showed up. I stayed. I persevered. If one artist left, I found another. Each wonderful in their own way, they came.

My mom adored Seth. She was a bright, vibrant, charismatic woman. She was the director of education for the New York City branch of the National Council of Jewish Women and was responsible for educating six thousand women. My mom worked until she retired at fifty-five. After

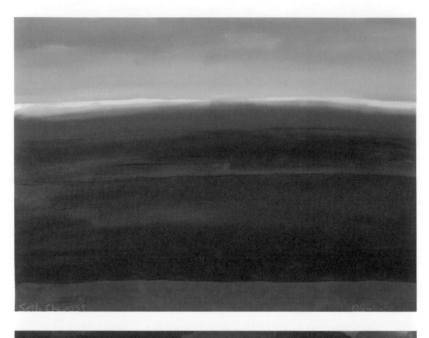

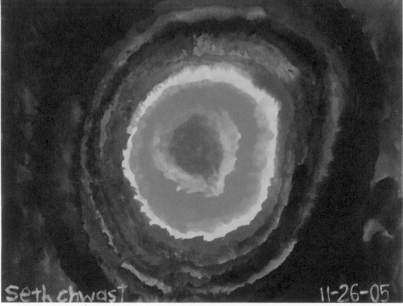

ABOVE: *Large Gradations—May 18, 2005*, 2005. Watercolor on paper, 21.5 × 29.25 inches.

RIGHT: *Circular Gradations—Nov. 26, 2005*, 2005. Watercolor on paper, 12 × 15 inches.

that, she read two books a day and immersed herself in appreciating music, art, travel, and volunteer work until we lost her at age seventy-six, when Seth was eight.

My mom embraced Seth. She sat on the floor and played with him, went to watch all his therapies, learned how to reinforce him, pushed me to push him, and showered him with gifts. She was the perfect grandmother. Besides visiting them in Florida, we took him to New York when they were there once or twice a year. They came to Cleveland for long weekends. After the car crash, Seth fell apart. He cried for about two hours a day. "Nana smash. Nana crash. Nana on Venus. Nana boom. Nana gone." His mourning went on for months. I had my pain. And I had his pain. As much as I wished I could take away Seth's pain, I was both stunned and comforted by the intensity of his grief. I took it as a good sign that Seth, despite his autism, could form close relationships and was saddened by the loss of that connection. I don't know why Seth reacted to my mom's death the way he did. I don't know what he understands about death or loss. Perhaps he felt her loss keenly because it was sudden, she didn't look old or ill, and he had a loving relationship with her. I do know he wasn't ready for his Nana to leave (and go to Venus). She was gone and he was bereft.

I am not alone. I am sustained by a circle of friends.

I have friends and I love them, but one day I thought about the future and understood that I needed new friends, more friends, friends who were smack in the middle of the age difference between me and my son. There are people my age and people his age who love him and care. The people my age may not be around long enough. The people his age may not have enough perspective. I found Ann Kocks, an angel who is seventeen years older than Seth and like a daughter to me. There could almost be another generation between me and my son. Searching for that middle generation was one of my best decisions. Opening my heart to Ann, allowing friendship to ignite into love, and refusing to let biology define family changed my life.

Although it was hard for me to pose the question, one day I asked Ann if she and her husband, Ken, would be willing to take Seth someday if the time came. Ann said she was totally open to it but would need to talk it over with Ken. His response: "Debra is like your mom, why wouldn't we take Seth?" When they came over to tell me their decision, my world changed from black and white to Technicolor. I assured them that I knew the enormity of what they had accepted to do and that we would review the decision each year in the event that their circumstances changed. Once we spoke, an enormous weight lifted off my shoulders. I was filled with peace and lost a tension so deep and pervasive that I hardly knew it was there until it was gone. My deepest worry was how to protect Seth after I was gone. I spend innumerable hours each day

RIGHT: *Central Park Horse's Carriage with Grayish-Purple Pinto Fantasy Horse*, 2007. Acrylic on canvas, 52 × 62 inches.

The Horse's carriage is Burgundy. The Horse has different Shapes of Spots. The stones are coffee and cream. The stones have rough and smooth Textures! The Horse's Head wears a Mask! I feel Proud and Enthusiastic! The Lamp was made out of steel and Glass. The Light is Yellow-Green. The Bucket is for Horse's Food. The Horse Feels Glad! The Painting is Beautiful!

making him laugh, playing silly games, and singing our songs. The remainder of my time is filled with creating a world for Seth, planning exhibitions, talking, e-mailing, writing, connecting with mentors, and bringing him and his art out into the world. Who else would do that? What would happen once I was gone? And then Ann changed my life and became both Seth's mother and my daughter. Seth says, "I have two moms." This is heaven on earth.

ABOVE: *The Village: Taxi Cab*, 2008. Acrylic on wood cutout, 5 × 4.5 × 5.5 inches.

Pleasure pours in from Ann, my new family, and from the energy of my parents who are long gone. Yes, I always feel their presence. I am living my dreams and my parents' dreams as we travel to New York and out into the world.

When I return to New York I feel my mother's energy. I feel her joy. I know how thrilled she would be to see Seth happily painting. And as Francis helps Seth, I feel my father. He loved Francis. In his heart, Francis was his son. To have Francis and Perry help Seth would be my dad's ultimate pleasure. I feel his joy. So whether we are packing for New York or Galapagos, I am crossing barriers of time and space, I am returning to the city where I grew up and I am going to Ecuador, the country whose very name means "the equator," a place that existed only in my dreams. I have moved from a closed, dark world to an open, green world where anything can happen. If a place can be an angel, New York is ours.

I WAS LUCKY TO FIND JOE, the composition major, who came into our lives in 2001, when Seth was eighteen. I met him through Becky, the artist who had arrived a few months earlier. On the first day the two met,

Joe came to me hours after working with Seth and said, "I'm jealous! I never met anyone with more raw talent!" Joe was intrigued with Seth and took him into his life. Everyone at the Cleveland Institute of Music gives a junior and a senior recital. They rehearse nightly for weeks and then perform. Joe took Seth to rehearsals in the afternoon and then out to dinner with the students in the evening. They would go to the recitals and to the parties after the recitals. Somehow people started to understand that Seth had unusual musical talents, and he started to find a world where he was recognized. Joe and Seth went to New York City to attend opera at the Met and concerts at Carnegie Hall; they attended recitals at Julliard.

I was still married back then. We went to see the Cleveland Symphony Orchestra—twenty-six concerts a year. I wanted Seth's dad to take Seth instead of me, but he was worried that Seth might act inappropriately and disrupt the experience for others in the audience. So Joe brought Seth to the symphony. They went to many concerts until it was clear that Seth knew how to behave in that realm. Finally, I gave Seth my concert ticket so that he could go with his dad. Since then Seth has never missed a concert. Our seats were across the aisle from the music critic for the *Plain Dealer*. Years later, when I met him at a party, he was kind enough to say to me, "If I didn't see Seth, it wouldn't be a concert!"

As Seth grew older, finding peers for him was not easy. In the beginning, I could call my friends, who'd come to dinner and bring their kids. I had Kyle, the nanny, and Yreka, the wonder dog, and playmates who were simply part of life. As we struggled toward age twelve, however, kids were no longer so available. They had their own lives, friends, and schedules. Becky and Joe were the first mentors who were close to Seth's age. When they left, Seth was nineteen and had no obvious possibilities for future peer contact. I asked my friend and neighbor, Pam, who is a school psychologist, for help. Together we called the guidance counselors of every local private school. We asked if they would give high school seniors community service credit for spending time with Seth. In return, we would provide an orientation on autism and an orientation on Seth. We would provide opportunities for observing language and music therapy. It would be educational. The students could come in groups of two or three if that would help them feel more comfortable.

Boy, did this idea ever work! Thirty-one kids signed up. Seventeen of them became regulars. I had to have one calendar dedicated to scheduling peer time for Seth. We did this for three years. Each year the program became more popular. The guidance counselors came to know us; the seniors would tell the juniors; and over time, we learned how to make it more rewarding for them.

David Cicerchi was one of our favorite peer volunteers. He spent his high school summers and vacations flying to South America to do service. During the school year he took Seth into his home and into his life. David stayed close to Seth the four years when he was in college and continued to be a part of Seth's life after he graduated. They would go to movies and concerts and take long walks. David included Seth in family parties and holiday traditions like baking Christmas cookies. He would pick up Seth and take him to his house for dinner and they would watch a video together. In 2007 he helped us take Seth to Costa Rica. All of this from a phone call to David's school in 2001! Another student, Emma, gave her senior talk on working with Seth. She went off to college in Montreal, where she majored in art history. When she returned to Cleveland after college, she came to visit Seth and saw his art: She was so moved that she wept. She remains in touch with Seth, attending his openings and taking him to concerts.

The program worked because it served a real need. Seth was desperate for friends, and each school had a community service requirement. One year a guidance counselor from one of the schools called. She said they planned to give their school's service award to the student who worked the most with Seth. She told me, "Lots of students pile up hours, but they're stuffing envelopes. It means nothing. But when they work with Seth, they can change his life. This is what we dream of when we ask our kids to perform service." It's what I dream of, also. Thank you, world! I am sorry I did not figure this out sooner. This is an idea that might work for any family in any community.

I continued the school volunteer program for three years. I stopped because the high school seniors were eighteen and Seth was now twenty-one and no longer interested. Seth's idea was to surround himself with people whom he calls "same-age"—which for him can mean anyone from twenty-one to forty. At this point that meant finding college-age students. I was not sure how to arrange this. Once again the universe helped, because soon David showed up with art students from the Cleveland Institute of Art who were all Seth's age. There is always a tension between protecting Seth because, on some levels, he cannot do what a twelve-year-old or even a five-year-old can do—yet one needs to respect that he is a man and has a right to make his own decisions. None of the people in my world let Seth eat foods that will make him ill. No matter how much he wants them. Aside from food, we try to let him make most choices. When he said, "No more high school seniors," that was that. I have to continually rethink my vision of him and keep encouraging him to grow and change.

Within a week after Seth appeared on the *Today* show, he had ten e-mail buddies who admired his art, and he became (for Seth) quite close with some of them. A favorite is Adam. Adam writes. Seth responds. Adam told Seth that Seth's e-mail is Adam's all-time favorite letter. He has an autistic nephew. Seth asked where Adam lives. Adam sent Seth a T-shirt of the lake he lives on in central Massachusetts, Lake

Chargoggagoggmanchauggagoggchaubunagungamaugg, an Indian name (and the longest place name in the United States) that is said to mean something like, "Settlers fish your pond, Indians fish our pond, and no one fishes the sacred middle pond." Seth, who loves geography, was thrilled. When Seth had an opening in New Jersey, Adam drove from outside of Boston to meet him. Before this, Seth had few friends. He had his artist mentors, who deeply cared about him. He had student volunteers. Some of my friends were kind enough to write. But now, for the first time, people we have never met want to contact Seth and correspond with him. Seth won't write e-mails unless I sit next to him. So we do it together. Seth does all the typing. I help with the words— and I mean major help. The only writing Seth does that is 100 percent Seth is his artist statements. Those pour out. I am careful to make sure people know their mail is from "Seth and Debra, the mom." For the first time in his life, Seth has a steady stream of mail.

Excited by his new e-mail friends and the three new Cleveland Institute of Art mentors, Seth started the *Fantasy Griffin* series with Janet, the *Fantasy Pegasus* series with Kathe, and *Blue Whales* with Jen Marie. The house exploded into color and joy. My goal was to have someone here whenever Seth wants to paint. And Seth often wants to paint! So, here we are. I have a son who is incredibly happy. It's not the

Big Whale Up Close, 2007. Oil on canvas, 24 × 90 inches.

happy ending I had dreamed of and hoped for, but it is happiness beyond anything I could have imagined.

People have asked me, "How do you find such wonderful mentors?" I believe the universe sends people who function like angels, people who are like blinking lights, who call to us, "Come to me. Look at me. Come this way." And they make a trail that could light up the night sky. Finding and following that trail is the work of the soul. The work of the body, the ego, is to get out of the way and let it happen.

How do any of us keep going when the road is hard, there is little support, and the odds are against us? I think the answer is the angels who provide support in unexpected ways. They seem to drop from the heavens and give generously of themselves. How do they do it? How do they slip beyond Seth's inability to have a conversation and touch his quick mind, his humor, and his desire to connect? When Seth was about eight, we flew into Boston to visit Kathy and Ray, good friends of ours who left Cleveland when Seth was two. Ray had been in the computer department at Case. Ray sat down with Seth and together they created a roller coaster, Strible Thrible, on the computer. Seth picked all the details: height, velocity, the number of drops, and their location. In the end, Strible Thrible threw riders wearing life jackets into the ocean and a helicopter picked them up. Ray, on the spot, created a web page for Strible Thrible so Seth could visit it on his computer. For Seth, this was a gift beyond rubies and diamonds. (In 2010, he painted this coaster in *Manhattan Floating*.)

In 2008, when we were at the Art Omi Residency in Ghent, Elisabeth Akkerman, the curator for the Francis J. Greenburger collection, was there and we had dinner with her one night. Elisabeth is from Germany. Seth loves geography. Elisabeth asked Seth the capital of a state. As we ate, she asked him the capital of every state. She would name a state; Seth would blurt out the capital. At the beginning, Seth answered and named an adjacent state. But Elisabeth said, "No, Seth. I have to think of the state." He gazed at her, mesmerized, waiting for her to remember each one. At the end, there was one missing. So she asked Seth for help. He whispered the last state. She said it out loud. He named the capital. While it may not seem like much, this was as close to a real conversation as I'd ever seen Seth engage in with anyone.

Ann Kocks, too, has the ability to get him to talk. She listens while Seth pours out roller coaster facts or updates on planned construction around town. She asks follow-up questions. Most people are confused about Seth's fascination with roller coaster facts and just tolerate it or try to change the topic. Ann engages him and turns it into a conversation. Ann often says, "He cracks me up." She enjoys Seth. He knows this. People find their own way to link to Seth. They go beyond language. I cherish every person who connects to my son.

I am encouraged by the number of total strangers who are inspired by Seth. Gretchen, a teacher, e-mailed Seth and we corresponded for a few months. Then she came to one of Seth's openings and I found myself holding hands with her as she told me about her five-year-old autistic grand-nephew, how hard their family tries, and how Seth is such a hope, such an inspiration. She cried as she was talking. And she wanted to know if she could write about him.

Someone else, a friend who is a therapist with a brain-damaged client, told her client about Seth. That woman now speaks about him weekly in therapy, follows his website, and wants to work on writing her own story. Seth has his own world. He has fans who love his art and fans who know little about art. But they all love his story.

How does Seth enchant people? I don't know. Maybe they are drawn to the gradations of color in *Four Fantasy Tree Frogs on a Yellow to Red Gradation,* or the wild mane of *Red Fantasy Horse's Head with Neck and Blue and Yellow Mane. The Big Orange Fantasy Horse* seems so friendly. *The*

RIGHT: *The Big Orange Fantasy Horse with Yellow Mane & Tail & Red Hooves & Blue Eyes with Navy Iris*, 2007. White oven-baked clay with acrylic paint, 14 × 17 × 5 inches.

BOTTOM: *Red Fantasy Horse's Head with Neck and Blue and Yellow Mane*, 2008. White oven-baked clay with acrylic paint, 8 × 8 × 3.5 inches.

The Horse's Head has Different Hues of Reds, Alizarin Crimsons, Ketchups, Pizza Sauces, Tomato Sauces, Tomato Soups, Candy Canes, and Candy Apples. The Eyes are Dark Blue and White. The Nose is Different Hues of Dark Blues and Dark Purples. The Mane has Different Hues of Blues, Sky Blues, Yellows, Yellow Sunflowers, Macaroni and Cheeses, and Cheese Sauces. The Horse feel thrilled. I feel enthusiastic.

OPPOSITE: *Four Fantasy Tree Frogs on a Yellow to Red Gradation*, 2007. Oil on canvas, 24 × 18 inches.

Trinidad Highway with Mountains, Houses, and Trees is so inviting.

Seth says, "New friends are everywhere." He runs up to random strangers and says, "What is your name? How old are you?" (This method does not go over so well with women over age twenty-seven.) We've learned to intervene and say, "This is Seth. He is an artist. He is autistic and working on his social skills." Then they either walk away or relax and chat awhile. Once when we were in the Houston airport, Seth ran up to a woman we did not know, lifted his sweatshirt, and showed her his T-shirt, which had a photo transfer of one of his paintings. She exclaimed, "I know you. You were on the *Today* show! I remember your face!" This was eleven months after he was on the show. We were amazed. She told us she was from Virginia and she took the time to speak to Seth. He flew home in a state of happiness.

When we landed in Cleveland, the man who helped us get our luggage looked at my shirt (I had put on the T-shirt with Seth's painting) and said, "That's Seth. I love his art." Another stranger recognized his art! I said I was his mom. He said, "Is he here? I want to meet him." Seth has become a first name. Strangers say, "That's Seth." Seth is right: New friends are everywhere.

The Trinidad Highway with Mountains, Houses, and Trees, 2009. Oil on paper, 18 × 24 inches.

The Highway has Different Tones of Gray with Line Marks have Different Hues of Yellows and Yellow School Buses. The Ground has Different Hues of Peanut Butters, Peanut Brittles, Cashew Crunches, Peanut Shells, Caramels, and Caramel Apples. The Trees have Different Hues of Purples, Violets, Greens, Teal Greens, Electric Lime Greens, Lime Greens, Green Grapes, Green Salads, Green Peppers, Green Cake Frostings, Green Apples, Light Greens, Dark Greens, and Green Grasses. The Houses are Different Hues of Yellows, Yellow School Buses, Pink Roses, Reds, Purples, and Turquoises. The Mountains have Different Hues of Purples, Violets, Purple Pansies, Purple Grapes, Teals, Teal Greens, Turquoise-Teals, Turquoises, and Blues. The Sky has Different Hues of Blues and Light Blues. The Clouds have Different Hues of Light Blues, Whites, and Blues. I feel thrilled about this painting.

CHAPTER 5

In Darwin's FootSteps

Our life changed when we went to Costa Rica in early 2007. It was Seth's first trip outside of North America and our first trip with Ann and her family. It was wonderful. After we got home, Seth said, "Galapagos." With that one word, our reality changed. Costa Rica was exotic. Galapagos is the place of dreams. Or the place beyond dreams—the Enchanted Islands. After seeing how the tropics transformed Seth's art, I knew we had to go. By Thanksgiving 2007, we were in the Galapagos, stepping over sea lions, dancing with the blue-footed boobies, searching for green sea turtles, and seeing the world that Darwin had seen more than 175 years ago. It felt otherworldly. It felt like home. We were in love. Four days after we returned from the trip, we had an offer for Seth to open at the John Madejski Gallery at the Royal Palm in Galapagos in late March 2008. Our life was set. We planned to return to Galapagos with Ann and her family next spring. Until then, Seth could paint icons of Galapagos nonstop. So I thought.

But Seth said, "Cayman Islands. We will go to Cayman Islands." Could we do it? It was January 15, 2008, late at night. We had to be home by February 12 for Seth's opening at Cleveland State University. Seth was insistent. He was painting for Galapagos day and night. A six-day break would not hurt us.

On the sixteenth, I got up at 6:00 a.m. and called a major international hotel chain and booked rooms on Grand Cayman. For Little Cayman I had no names, numbers, or any way of reaching resorts. After a quick visit to the bookstore to do some research, I called the Southern Cross Club, named for the constellation. It is primarily a dive resort. People also go there to fish. We do neither. The concierge

Blue-Headed Bird in the Rain Forest, 2007. Oil on canvas, 48 × 36 inches.

reassured us, helped us organize, and arranged our plane flights. By three in the afternoon we were fully booked for three days in Grand Cayman and three days in Little Cayman.

I spent the next day planning. We would go to Stingray City and swim with the stingrays. One tour makes two stops to snorkel on the way. Never mind that we have never snorkeled before. We also booked the Atlantis submarine, which goes down one hundred feet and would let Seth relax and simply watch fish without any effort. In the Cayman guidebook, under Art Galleries, I found the National Gallery of the Cayman Islands, a nonprofit interested in education. I called and asked for their curator, and spoke with Natalie Coleman, who agreed to meet us the day after we arrived.

We loved the National Gallery. Exhibits run for several months and they provide on-going educational classes. They have a clear mission. Our timing was perfect. Natalie loved Seth's work and wanted to present him and his story to the gallery planning committee. The only catch was that the paintings had to portray Cayman, which was fine with us.

After the gallery we headed to the Atlantis dock where Seth went into high gear, stopping everyone he saw, showing his T-shirt with the photo transfer of his work, giving out cards, asking for everyone's e-mail. Let me be clear: Seth was not selling. He has almost no concept of money. He was looking for friendship. Has he ever had a true friend? I cannot begin to understand what friendship means to Seth. You are his friend if you e-mail him and, maybe, if you simply take his card. Maybe it is enough if you tell him your name and where you live. Then Seth will gaze at you with intensity and say, "New friends are everywhere." Someday this may expand to something more reciprocal. Right now Seth is searching for friends. In his world anyone who will stop and speak with him is a friend.

In Darwin's Footsteps

We got on the boat that takes tourists to the submarine; there were maybe twenty people who came along for a ten-minute ride. Seth continued giving out cards, showing his shirt, and asking for names of children and grandchildren. For the first time in my travels with Seth I felt the need to make an announcement to a group. I introduced and explained Seth to everybody. One man approached me; a cantor for a reform temple in Westchester who works with several autistic kids. He asked if Seth would consider coming to New York to show his art and then I could give a talk. The cantor thought the kids he works with would like this. Seth's response was, "Grow your brain. New friends are everywhere."

The next day we were on our way to Stingray City. For the two snorkeling stops, the guides were friendly, competent, and patient as, knowing nothing, we plunged in. The fish were everywhere, a garden of beautiful moving colors. When we drifted too far, they threw life rings to us and pulled us back to the boat.

14 Fishes, 2008. Acrylic on canvas, 16 × 34 inches.

The Fishes feel comfort. The Ocean is The Fishes' Home. I visited the Beautiful Fish. The Stones are on the Beach. The Beach is hot! The Sand and Stones have texture. The Stones have Different Hues of Yellows, Greens, and Golds. The Clouds are fluffy. The Schools of Fishes are swimming! The Fish are exciting to me! Some Fishes have scales. The scales protect their Bodies. The scales are shiny. I feel proud!

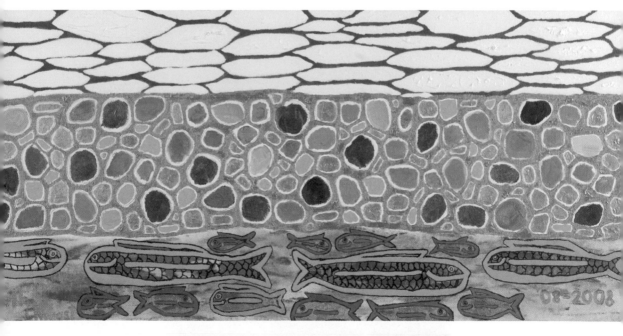

The third stop was Stingray City. Historically, fishermen cleaned fish here, throwing scraps overboard, and the stingrays came to feed. These stingrays are tame and plentiful. As we pulled up, the water was filled with huge, dark shapes. They know tourist boats bring food. We picked the "stand in four feet of water" option with no snorkeling, which entailed simply getting in the water and, for me, screaming as the stingrays glide around our bodies feeling like velvet—friendly, but unpredictable, velvet.

Seth immediately knew what to do. He didn't want to step on the stingrays or be surprised by their movement. He jumped in my arms, all six feet of him, grabbed onto my neck, and laughed the whole time. Somehow in the buoyancy of the saltwater I could hold Seth in my arms while we felt the stingrays move around us. It was amazing and unforgettable. The guides held the stingrays while we stroked

RIGHT: *The Spotted Eagle Ray*, 2008. Oil on canvas, 48 × 48 inches.

The Spotted Eagle Ray has different Tones of Gray and White. The Spotted Eagle Ray has Donuts, Dots, and Imaginary Shapes on his body. It is a Boy. It was easy to do the shapes. I like shapes and patterns. The water has Spotted Eagle Ray. The Spotted Eagle Ray feels Calm and Comfort. I feel happy about this painting.

LEFT: *The Great Blue Heron Head*, 2008. Oil on canvas, 15.5 × 19.25 inches.

them. They gave people chopped fish to feed them. We were covered in stingrays and oh, so happy.

The next day we flew to Little Cayman. The airport and the fire department share one building. The island is ten miles long by one mile wide and there are about 150 people living there year-round. When the tourists come (and they come in droves), they double the island's population. The bank is open for two hours twice a week. There is one school for grades one to six with four children. We came to see the blue of the sky, the color of the sea, and the frigate birds, which are huge and fly overhead all day. During mating season the males inflate the immense scarlet courting pouches on their throats. It was amazing to see these midnight black birds with their ruby throats. We loved the warm beach, the colors of the water, and the glorious sunsets. The first night, Seth yelled, "Stars!" We looked up and saw a sky so populated with stars that we could not believe it was real.

We stayed in a resort with twelve rooms and twenty-four guests. There were no room keys and no one wore shoes. While other guests were out scuba diving and fishing, we lay in hammocks, watching the

The Great Blue Heron has many Different Hues of Browns, Creams, Rusty Oranges, Chocolates, Terra Rosa Hues, Grays, Yellows, Peaches, Peanut Butters, Peanut Shells, Cashew Crunches, Peanut Brittles, Wheat Colors, Caramels, Butterscotches, Maple Syrups, Pumpkins, Burnt Umbers, Burnt Siennas, Moonlights, Blacks, Tans, Coffees, Pinks, Apricots, and White. The Background has many Different Hues of Reds, Mangoes, Guavas, Papayas, Oranges, Tangerines, Apricots, Yellows, Terra Rosa Hues, Rose Madder Hues, and Pumpkins. The Bird feels calm and comfort. I feel enthusiastic. I love the Great Blue Heron.

changing color of the sea. Every day at four in the afternoon a great blue heron landed in front of us and walked back and forth in the water fishing. There is a tiny island, Owens Island, located two hundred yards away from the resort. One day a guide took us there snorkeling. He spotted a baby stingray. We didn't see it but Seth wouldn't stop hoping and looking. He kept asking, "Where is baby stingray?" and going back under.

We flew home, already longing to return to Cayman. Back in the States, Cleveland State University had started the Common Reading Experience 2008. The first book was Mark Haddon's *The Curious Incident of the Dog in the Night-Time*. It is a mystery with a mathematically gifted autistic teenage protagonist. The university students were encouraged to read it, along with thousands of other American college students. The university asked for Seth's art to be in the library for all of February and for me to talk about the book during one lunch period. We talked to a standing-room-only crowd. All the students wanted to meet Seth, and he gave his card to everyone. His second nanny, Lisa, was there. She left when she was twenty-two. Now she was thirty. Where did the time go? She cried and told Seth that she has a scrapbook with all of his newspaper clippings.

WE WROTE TO GRAHAM WATKINS, director of the Charles Darwin Foundation and told him we would be coming to the Galapagos for Seth to have an exhibition. He was welcoming and friendly and wanted to meet us. In November 2007 we began preparing for the exhibition in Galapagos at the Royal Palm. I called the woman who ships for us locally and asked, "Can you ship to Galapagos?" I explained that the art would need to fly to Houston, then to Quito, Ecuador, and then Baltra—the last of which also involved a boat ride to the island of Santa Cruz, and then a drive to the Royal Palm. There was dead silence at the other end of the line. Three days later she called back and said, "Do not do it."

Vasco, the curator of the gallery at the Royal Palm, wrote and also said, "Don't ship!" He suggested that we take the paintings apart, bring the unstretched canvases, and he would have stretchers built in Santa Cruz. I found myself apologizing for my endless questions and explained that we have never had an international opening. He replied, "Neither have I!" He was moved by Seth's art and story and wanted to do it. We all meant well. We were all competent. And none of us knew exactly what we were doing! All of us being in the same boat of ignorance relaxed me.

Bill Lynerd is a neighbor and the head of development of the Cleveland Museum of Natural History. A few days before our departure, in the middle of the night, I thought, *Galapagos—Darwin—natural history—Bill should see these paintings.* The problem was they were already at UPS (they were professionally packing them for us to carry on the plane). The next day, though, UPS told me that the canvases were too large to pack. We had to take them all home and fold back the edges to meet the 62-inch length limit for airline regulations. Luckily, because we had to bring the art home, Bill was able to run over and see the originals. On the spot he exclaimed that he wanted to show Seth's work. By Monday morning Bill met with everyone on the exhibit committee. In the spring of 2009 they would be celebrating Darwin's two hundredth birthday. Would Seth be the artist for their Darwin exhibition? Yes! That same Monday morning, the Royal Palm called, frantic, as the shipment was now running late. I felt pressured, mortified, and inadequate.

Suddenly I knew that I would never do last-minute pressured packing again. Our next opening, if we got it, would be in Cayman. I decided that three weeks before the art had to leave Cleveland, Seth would stop painting. We would go out to dinner, celebrate, and give ourselves three weeks to pack. We would stroll into UPS and say, "Here it is. Send it

This Tortoise is very old. I saw this Tortoise at the Charles Darwin Foundation. The Tortoise has Different Hues of Chocolates, Coffees, Greens, Turquoises, Reds, Rose Madder Hues, Whites, Peaches, Yellows, Tans, Browns, Grays, Green Olives, Cucumbers, Zucchinis, Pickles, Oranges, Peaches, Creams, Terra Rosa Hues, Blacks, Peanut Shells, Grapefruits, and White. The Sky has Different Hues of Blues, Creams, Grays, and Whites. The Tortoise feels comfort, calm and relaxed. The Tortoise feels safe. I feel thrilled. I love This Tortoise. I love Galapagos.

Seth Chwast

03-19-2008

off." If Seth had just started his "best" Cayman painting, he could finish it later, but not for that exhibition! That was my fantasy about how it would happen next time. But first we had to get to Galapagos.

Until then I would do anything, accept any chance for publicity, exposure, adventure. We had nothing to lose. What was the alternative? A career in dry mopping? I followed every lead, hoping the universe would take us someplace wonderful. Or at least to safety. Seth painted until the last minute because each painting was so beautiful, and I so desperately wanted it to be a great exhibition. Now I understood that Seth was visible. We would not be begging, hoping, and praying for openings. We were opening in Galapagos. And maybe in Cayman. We could slow down and smell the roses even as the universe sped up around us and there were more and more demands on Seth's time and art.

I wanted Galapagos to be the best opening possible. We decided to make a poster combining four of Seth's paintings of four sea lions. I ordered one hundred and got one thousand. I probably needed a thousand and didn't know it. I packed 120 of the Seth T-shirts that we wear when we travel to give away. I loved *The Giant Fantasy Tortoise*, the final painting that held up our packing at UPS. It could have gone into the next exhibition.

As things became less frantic, I believed there would be a next time. I had lived in fear so long that I could scarcely believe we had found safety. Picture me, afraid to die because no one would see and know that Seth is wonderful, special, funny, bright, and gifted. Now here he was, revealed for all to see.

On Wednesday, March 26, we flew to Ecuador along with our beloved Kocks/Perelman family. As we landed in Galapagos, once again I felt like our life was about to change.

When we got to the Royal Palm, everything was just about ready. The carpenters had built the stretchers; all that needed to be done was to staple the canvases onto them, so we left to meet Graham Watkins of the Charles Darwin Foundation.

Graham told that us he was moving on from the foundation at the end of the year, and was thinking of going to Africa. He mentioned that Seth might like painting African animals. I realized that Seth may have just been invited to paint in Africa! We were no longer in Kansas.

We went to lunch in town where sea lions lie on the park benches and pelicans sit in the fountains. We sat by them and took photos. The pelicans did not pay any attention to us, they just stretched their wings and dipped their beaks into the water.

Later we returned to the Royal Palm. All the paintings had been hung. Imagine a large circular room with white walls. The floor is made of large lapis lazuli blue tiles. The ceiling is like a jungle hut; an inverted ice cream cone reaching toward the sky. The windows are circular, and every ten feet there is a half of a tree trunk in the wall, breaking the wall into units. Each section had two of Seth's paintings. A wooden shelf arcing along one wall held his sea lion and tortoise sculptures. There was

ABOVE: *Lonesome George B: Dark Green on Shell, Purple on Skin and Multicolor Specks on Legs*, 2009. White oven-baked clay with acrylic paint, 6 × 12 × 6 inches.

a table for the posters and T-shirts and four pedestals with flowers. Seth jumped and laughed and ran in place. We took Seth's artist statements and taped each one under the right painting. We were in a dream.

The opening was that evening. We were told that the Royal Palm would try to have 40 or 50 people come to the gallery, but discovered that they had invited 150 people, including the mayor and governor of Galapagos. National TV was there. Would I be willing to speak on television? As I talked, Roberto Nappe, who supervised the opening, translated into Spanish. He spoke with profound emotion and love. I was transfixed by his face and by his words. Although I do not understand Spanish, I do understand love.

The room filled with people we met on our first trip (our guide, Yvonne, gallery owners), people from the Darwin Foundation, and people we didn't yet know—mothers, writers, travelers, photographers, sailors, and reporters. They invited the only special needs teacher in Galapagos. She spoke to me in Spanish with Roberto translating, saying she was a teacher, not a special education teacher. She had five autistic students. Could I help her? One of the students was there, a lovely young woman who was crying. Her father was also crying. They were overwhelmed by who Seth was (he has less language than the young woman) and what he had accomplished. They were filled with pride and hope. Roberto kept translating. Graham stayed close. He loved the art.

By 9:30 it was over. Roberto, the beautiful gallery, the three professional carpenters (one of whom was an artist), the talks with Graham, lunch with the pelicans and the sea lions on the park benches, being with Ann and her family on Galapagos, the beauty of the exhibition, and the party all seemed to swirl around in my head. I was having trouble believing it or understanding how it all came to be. Who is Seth? How did this happen?

In Darwin's Footsteps

I would like to say something else about the Galapagos trip. By the end of our time there, Seth seemed less autistic. Let me clarify. He was still plenty autistic, but it seemed to me that he was a little less so.

One night on the boat I asked Seth what we did that day. I had a pad and wrote down what he said. Here it is:

We went to the Isabel Islands and people jumped and people dived into the Pacific Ocean and snorkeled and to see the giant sea turtle. We went to the hidden cave with wave sounds and people stays on the raft with sea turtles, blue-footed boobies, Sally Lightfoot crabs, penguins. We went to Fernandina Island in the morning. We saw iguanas. We saw Lightfoot crabs, sea lions. We went to across the equator. We wore costumes of pirates. King and queen. Children were off in costumes. Children jumped into the Jacuzzi. Children get out Jacuzzi, go down to third floor. Sidney did not wore a costume of pirates because Sidney was old. Hors d'oeuvres on third floor today.

Brief translation:

We did our first deep water snorkeling. We could not walk into the water from the shore. We had to slip off the boat into fifteen feet of water. That evening the ship crossed the equator. Two adult guests dressed as king and queen. All the young children, including Senna and Zander, dressed as pirates. Sidney, age twelve, did not.

Those are the facts of what happened; Seth's version is more poetic. The next day I again asked Seth what happened and this is what he said:

We dived into the Pacific Ocean. We saw different kinds of fish and colors. We went to Santa Cruz Island. Lights in the lava tunnel. We

TOP: *Blue-Footed Booby Is Standing on a Rock,* 2007. Oil on canvas, 24 × 18 inches.

Blue-footed Booby is standing on a Rock. The Booby has Blue Feet. The Rock has shiny with glitter. The Rock has rough and smooth. The Bird has Different Hues of Creams, Browns, Blues, Violets, Golds, and Black. The Bird's Head has shiny. The Bird feels glad and peaceful. My Friend Jonathan R. Green took a photograph of this Bird. I saw Many Blue-footed boobies sitting and standing and walking on the Galapagos Islands.

saw giant tortoises. We heard the rain with thunderstorms. We got two shirts for Seth. We went to piano lounge. A man talked about tomorrow go back to Quito, Ecuador.

Hearing his take on what had transpired felt like being hit by lightning. For twenty-six years I had not known what Seth was aware of, absorbing, noticing, or contemplating. A recitation of what we did on that day may not seem significant, but it was much more than I had ever heard from Seth in the past. No, it wasn't philosophical or emotional and it was primarily visual, but in his descriptions of that day and the day before there were observations that I had not heard Seth share previously. His description included sounds, it included reasoning. Younger children were in costume. Sidney was not. No one explained to him that she thought she was too old for dressing up. Seth, correctly, understood this and bothered to describe it. This was a first.

I have a memory of only one time when Seth volunteered words when he was around ten years old. I was so shocked I wrote it down: "Insects have no legs, no arms, no teeth, no tongue. Seth's body has no wings. Seth has no horns. Animals have horns. A bull. French horn is a horn in France, in forest, in country." What a mystery our world and our language must be for Seth. It is amazing he even tries. These were free associations giving a glimpse of how words and thoughts run through Seth's mind. But in Galapagos, he dived both into the ocean and into words.

Seth is not silent. He makes happy sounds. He hums. He uses words to let you know what he wants, to share roller coaster facts, to ask questions that interest him ("Where are your grandparents from?") or to comment on the universe ("New friends are everywhere." "Grow your brain."). I get information by asking a series of questions that require a one-word answer, which I may or may not get. Typically, Seth does not describe his day or share what he saw or heard. The dictations I

OPPOSITE BOTTOM: *Two Iguanas*, 2009. Oil on canvas, 30 × 40 inches.

The 2 Iguanas have many of colors. I painted 2 Iguanas in 250 hours. The 2 Iguanas are in Little Cayman in British West Indies. We saw Iguanas in Little Cayman. The Iguanas feel calm and comfort. I fed the bananas for Iguanas in Little Cayman. This painting is beautiful. This painting is easy. It took a long time. This painting goes to the Cleveland Museum of Natural History for July 18 to October 11, 2009. Prints and T-shirts will go to the National Trust of the Cayman Islands for the new Iguana Reserve.

transcribed in Galapagos were language, not speech. What mom of an autistic person expects a change in language at age twenty-six?

Until these two dictations about his day, Seth's only outpourings had been his artist statements. Those are pure Seth. They are primarily visual and literal. He simply names what is right in front of him. Seth loves to write artist statements. He looks at paintings and color words flow out of him. For example, this is his artist statement for his Galapagos poster of four sea lions:

> The 4 Squares of Sea Lions on poster. The Sea Lions are Colors of Lavender, Green, Hot Pink, & Turquoise. The Background has Colors of Purple, Blue, Teal & Pink. (The Turquoise Sea Lion with) The Purple Background has Pansies, Magentas, Maroons, Cherries, Grapes, Lilacs, Lavenders, & Plums. (The Lavender Sea Lion with) The Teal Background has Turquoises, Sages, Blue-Greens, Phthalo Greens, Oceans, Lakes, Ponds, Dark Greens, Prussian Blues, & Viridians. (The Hot Pink Sea Lion with) The Blue Background has Prussian Blues, French Ultramarines, Phthalo Blues, Cobalt Blues, Navy Blues, Blueberries, Blue Poppies, Oceans, Lakes, Blue Skies, Blue Jeans, Blue Plums, Blueberry Pies, Teals, Turquoises, American Ultramarines, Evening Blues, Dark Knight's Blues, & Waterfalls. (The Green Sea Lion with) The Pink Background has Strawberries, Raspberries, Cherries, Magentas, Violets, Valentine's Day Pinks, Red-Pinks, Pansies, Pink Roses, Strawberry Jellies, Strawberry Gelatins, Strawberry Butters, Dark Pinks, Light Pinks, Strawberry Cream Cheeses, Strawberry Cheesecakes, & Pink Fireworks.

Galapagos Poster, 2008.
Print on paper,
18 × 24 inches.

This is the peak of Seth's pre-Galapagos writing. It is evocative, creative, and poetic. What he told me about his day snorkeling and crossing the equator felt more like an exchange that could happen

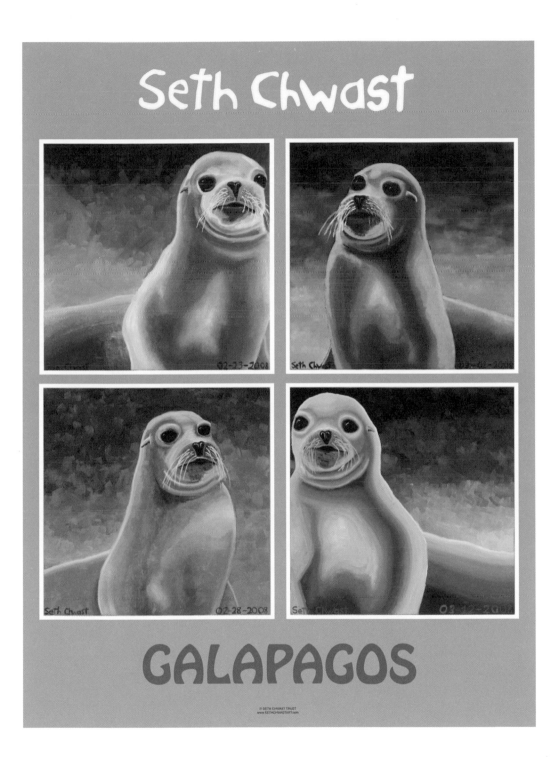

between two people anywhere. It is common to ask someone, "What did you do today?" It was amazing that Seth even answered the question when I asked him what we did. Most questions are met with silence or, at best, silence and a smile.

I accept Seth's non-responses because I don't hold him to the expectations of my world. In fact, I am more than willing to leave my world and enter his. I come in and make myself comfortable. I refuse to wonder what it would be like if I had a son who could speak. We relax into his world. We pushed language day and night for decades. I read the autism miracle cure books. One family does something and their child is now normal and you can do it, too. One child is cured. Following the same program, some families go from two-word sentences to five-word sentences. Some get no change. We got a lot of no change. Seth was born in 1983 and we first had access to a school that specialized in autism when he was eighteen. Maybe there is better help now. I am not a researcher or an expert. I'm a mom. We tried system after system from the time Seth was twenty-one months old until he was twenty-two years old to no avail. Having long given up on ever seeing any change in his functional speech, Seth had a significant breakthrough on the Galapagos Islands. He had crossed a line.

Perhaps something changed there for Seth because he was treated like a star. He was taken seriously by the external world. He saw his art in a beautiful gallery in a foreign country. He knew he was on national television. The staff on the boat called him by name and fussed over him on his birthday. We showed prints of his Galapagos paintings to people who were blown away. Maybe our world finally showed enough interest in him for him to feel safe, curious, and/or motivated enough to leave his world and test the waters. Something shifted. I know this process started with his first painting in 2003, but perhaps it had finally built enough momentum to make a difference. Maybe when your mom likes a painting, that is well and good, but when there is a party for 150 people and national TV is there and everybody is talking to you, it may bring about change.

Darwin created a template for the study of evolution: passion, perseverance, hard work, attention to detail, an open mind, a willingness to give up assumptions in the face of new information. Seth is leading me through a similar but more personal evolution. First I tried to bring him into our world. Now I try to go into his. There is some flow back and forth. Now he is a bit more in mine. Both Graham Watkins from the Charles Darwin Foundation and Bill Lynerd from the Cleveland Museum of Natural History really like Seth. Maybe the natural history people have a curiosity and a delight in someone who is a bit different and wonderful.

TRAVELING IN ECUADOR, we all wore T-shirts with photo transfers of Seth's paintings. One depicts an apricot Pegasus flying into the stars. Another has beautiful twin horses, a teal horse on a lavender background and a lavender horse on a teal background. The third displays a grid of tiny horses, apricot and yellow with black manes, and spruce green with red manes; thirty tiny horses, each with its own smile and beautiful body. These stunning images served as visual aids. Seth would approach someone and pull up his sweatshirt as if to show his belly and there would be a Pegasus. I or one of our traveling companions would run over and say, "Seth is an artist. That is his painting. I'm wearing another one of his paintings." These images of his art gave Seth the best chance of having something that you and I take for granted. We can turn to any stranger and say, "What a hot day," or murmur, "Beautiful sunset," and we can connect. That connection confirms our existence. We all tend to catalog each other by age, clothing, appearance, the book we're carrying, or the dog we're walking. That cataloging can form the basis of a conversation

Orange Fantasy Pegasus #7 with Stars, 2007. Oil on canvas, 48 × 36 inches.

The Pegasus has Oranges and Yellows. The Background has many stars. The Sky has many Blues. The Stars are 2 Yellows and Gold. The mane is Yellow. The Horse feels happy. The texture is smooth.

that sometimes builds into a relationship. We can chat in the moment or move on, but for a time we are a part of someone else's life. Seth never has that chance. Seth making any type of contact, even with his mom's help rushing in to explain, was the high point of his social life.

It can be painful to see Seth out in the world; my heart aches when I think about my son asking random people for their e-mail as they ignore him and walk away. This time, there was magic in the air. On the way home from Galapagos, in a shop in the Quito airport, a saleswoman who barely spoke English told me her son was like Seth. Her son was fourteen and autistic. The other saleslady came over to help interpret. I showed them our shirts and Seth's signature on the painting, pointing so they could see that Seth was the artist. Everything that troubled and pained me, all the ways that Seth does not and cannot pass for normal, were the lights that signaled to this mom that Seth was an autistic man. In seconds she knew. In seconds she also knew his art was spectacular. A minute later, after pointing and gesturing and me speaking English and her speaking Spanish, she was hugging me and we were both crying and she was patting Seth and murmuring to him in Spanish. And then she was glowing with joy and with hope. All because Seth does not and cannot "pass."

Red-Orange Self-Study with Horses and Striped Background, 2006. Acrylic on board, 15 × 30 inches.

The Grid has Background Colors. The Horses have Many of Colors. The Horses are Animation. The Horses are Walking. The Horse has Mane, Eye, Lips, Hooves, and Tail. The Horses feel Enthusiastic and Glad. I feel Thrilled. The Self-Study has Gradations from Dark to Light. The Self-Study has Many of Reds and Oranges. The Self-Study has Gradations of Hair and Face from Dark to Light. Half grid, half self-study same one. Smaller than the big canvas. Red-orange lights and darks. Details of horses have mane and tail, eyes, and lips. The background is lines in different colors. I like the painting—feels astonished.

On the flight from Quito to Houston, Seth was quiet. I would have said no one knew he was autistic. Within an hour, the stewardess was crouching by our side. She had an autistic ten-year-old son. More shirts, more business cards with *Big Red Orange Fantasy Horse*, more flyers with the *Green Apple Pinto Fantasy Horse*, *Big Red Fantasy Horse*, and *Blue-Headed Bird in the Rain Forest*. More tears. More hope.

We feel like we are following in Darwin's footsteps. Darwin set off in his twenties on his sea voyage on the *Beagle*, going from port to port for five years. Seth went to Costa Rica at twenty-four. Galapagos and Cayman were his next choices. We get many inquiries asking for Seth to come and paint. Currently, painting the dolphins of Curaçao is the

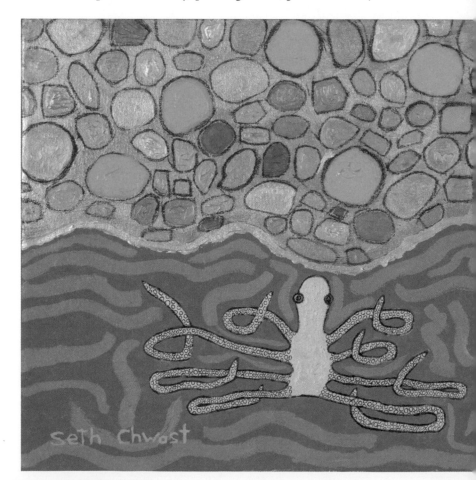

project he mentions most. He speaks of Malta and Greenland. Then I realize that *Manhattan Floating* is really a painting of an island. Two hundred years after Darwin, we are on our own path of discovery.

Our journey took us back to Cayman. *Seth Chwast: Visions of Cayman* was shown at the National Gallery of the Cayman Islands from October 25, 2008, to February 25, 2009. They exhibited thirty-three paintings. His name covered an entire wall. We flew down three times to do gallery tours, appear on local TV, meet with families of the autistic, and lead workshops for special needs staff. Seth was a hit. Everyone loved him. The curator bought a triptych (*Horizontal Purple Aurora Triptych with Rivers, Lakes, Deciduous* (see page 122) and *3 Giant Octopuses* for her

3 Giant Octopuses, 2008. Acrylic on canvas, 16 × 34 inches.

I used real rocks to draw. The Rocks are on the Beach are rough and smooth. The Rocks are different Hues of Golds, Yellow-oranges, and Greens. The Sand is White-Gold. The Ocean has different Hues of Blues. The Waves are different brush strokes. The 3 Octopuses' legs have tentacles. The Octopuses' bodies are rough and smooth. The Ocean is cool and warm Blues. The Ocean is very, very, very Huge! The Octopuses' Friend's are in the Ocean. I feel enthusiastic about this Painting! 3 Giant Octopuses was very hard to paint! This Painting grows your brain and grows your spirit! I feel happy and calm, about the Octopuses. The Octopuses feel excited, proud, and calm. This New Painting is Beautiful and Fantastic!

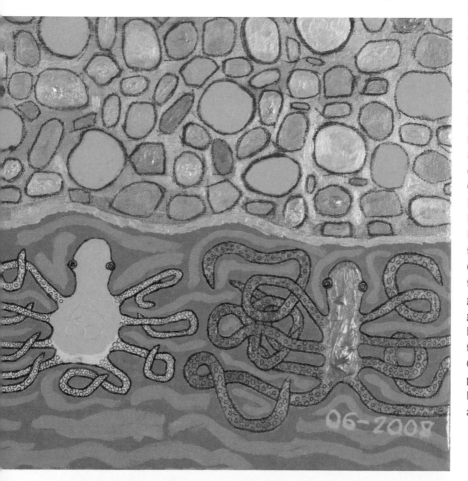

personal collection. In early February, the director semiretired to spend more time with her family. The gallery purchased *Twelve Griffins Over the Rain Forest in Costa Rica* (see page 49) as a thank-you gift for her, as they knew it was her favorite. These paintings and eight others now live in Cayman. Seth was most excited.

Karen Stary, the founder of the Dolphin Heart Foundation in the United States, sent an e-mail. She works with the Curaçao Dolphin Therapy and Research Center, an organization that provides dolphin therapy for special needs people, especially those challenged by autism, Down syndrome, and cerebral palsy. They are an agency with links to the United States, Holland, and Germany. Did Seth want to paint dolphins? she wanted to know. Our world was expanding.

Arielle Mark, an art consultant who owns an art gallery in Englewood, New Jersey, also e-mailed. Her assistant went to Cayman on vacation and saw Seth's art. Arielle invited us to have an exhibition in her gallery at the end of May 2009. E-mails flew back and forth as we tried to determine which paintings she wanted and what was available.

Seth was already scheduled for *Seth Chwast: A Retrospective* to open at the Jewish Community Center in Cleveland that May and for *Visions of Galapagos: The Inspired Works of Seth Chwast* at the Cleveland Museum of Natural History from July to October. The museum, of course, wanted the Galapagos paintings. The Mark Gallery wanted only paintings that were for sale, but they asked for some of our favorites that we were not ready to give up. The JCC wanted important paintings from each year. All three requested some of the same paintings. We sat down with all of the request lists and made charts, going over it again and again.

When I was told that my son was autistic, I could never have imagined that one of the challenges I would face would be trying to figure out where and when his paintings would appear. As problems go, I'll take it.

3 Swimming Turtles with Yellow Stones, 2008. Oil and acrylic on canvas, 60 × 36 inches.

Turtles feel happy swimming in the Ocean! The Turtles' Shells have different hues of Oranges, Golds, Greens, and Blues. The Turtles' Eyes are Gold and Dark Blue. The Turtles' Faces are Sage and Gold. The Turtles' Skin have scales on their Bodies. The Turtles' Shells are hard to Protect their Bodies. The Turtles' Shells have shapes and patterns with lines. The Rain Forest Leaves have veins. Some Leaves are Dark Purple with Gold. The Rain Forest Background has Different Hues of Greens. The Sky is above the Rain Forest. The Ocean is below the Rain Forest. The Ocean's Water is Cool. 3 Swimming Sea Turtles are Beautiful! I swim in the Ocean with 3 Sea Turtles! We have a lot of fun!

CHAPTER 6

Auras and Auroras

It's not the gardener who creates the garden—it's the garden that creates the gardener. Seth created me. He catapulted me into endurance, perseverance, problem solving, service, and finally into the spiritual. I spent a decade chasing every possibility, running around and searching everywhere for a miracle. And then, exhausted, I began a different kind of journey.

In 1995 Seth turned twelve and it was clear that there would not be a miracle. Back then we were told that if the autism was ever to normalize, it would happen by twelve. Seth is autistic and nothing that I have done, no amount of therapy, time, or money can change that. So here I am, a secular Jew from Brooklyn, and suddenly I am starting to contemplate my soul. I had always been interested in hypnosis, dreams, and spiritual journeys. Now the interest intensified. I started questioning everything: Could there be some other meaning to life? What does my soul want? Where is my soul? I'm still attached to my son; I love my son like I have never loved anyone. I will do anything for him, but we have ceased chasing something that cannot be caught. In terms of Seth acquiring functional language or somehow overcoming the autism, there's nothing left to chase. I didn't give up on Seth, we simply relaxed a little and stopped fighting so hard.

Suddenly, everything was okay. I don't mean the work was over. On some level, it had just begun. Seth would not be like other people. He would not wake up one day able to speak. I would need to keep fighting to create a good life for him—a different life, but a good life. And I would have to protect him beyond my own life. He would never be independent. I knew that I could not fail him.

OPPOSITE: *Imaginary Shapes of Northern Lights—Jan. 10, 2006*, 2006. Watercolor on paper, 11.5 × 8.25 inches.

After Seth turned twelve, I started to feel that I needed spirituality like I needed oxygen. When you exhaust everything in the real world, the world as you know it, you start to contemplate the moon and the stars, the flowers and the birds, until everything becomes a miracle. When you fully realize this, by grace you're in a different reality, where every breath is a gift and where you have a passion for the green of the grass and the blue of the sky. When the tension and pain and struggle have been burnt away, all that remains is the soul. And the soul doesn't care whether or not Seth goes to Harvard. The soul has a soft, quiet voice. It has to do with love and peace and living in the moment and forgetting about externals.

My ex-husband was the best dad of an autistic child. He loved and supported Seth, but when he told me that he had no interest in my spirituality, that was the beginning of the end of our marriage. He was

Many Imaginary Shapes Northern Lights, 2005. Oil on canvas, 48 × 60 inches.

The Imaginary Shapes have Different Hues of Oranges, Yellows, Purples, Blues, Reds, and Greens. The Deciduous Trees have Different Hues of Browns, Greens, and Yellow-Greens. The Pine Trees are behind the Deciduous Trees. The Pine Trees have Different Hues of Light Greens and Greens. The Snow-Capped Mountains have Different Hues of Purples, Blues, Violet-Blues, Light Blues, and Whites. The Sky is Nighttime. I like this painting.

on a different path, and we drifted apart. In that ending came a new beginning. Ultimately, I think that my spiritual quest gave me some of the strength required to accompany Seth on his journey.

After a while, I wandered into Kabbalah, Jewish mysticism. I started listening to teaching tapes of Rabbi David Zeller, a Jungian, singing, storytelling rabbi, who became a close friend until he passed away in 2007. In 2001 I found Rabbi Yitzchak Schwartz, a big bear of a country western–singing, open-minded, joyful Texan who had moved to Israel. He became my primary teacher. By 2003 we were studying Kabbalah by phone for five hours a week. He was coming to our home twice a year to give seminars to the community, and I was in prayer three hours a day. This stopped in 2007 when we started to travel and Seth's career exploded. Managing Seth's life became my spiritual path. Yitzchak will always be in my heart and Kabbalah is one of the ways I orient to the world.

In Kabbalah we learn that every person has a destiny. If you lead a good life and do everything right but never do what you were meant to do, your life is wasted. It sounds a little harsh but what if it is true for each of us? The hardest part, as far as I am concerned, is figuring out my destiny. Having a destiny sounds so large and grand and I am private, reclusive. I can spend ten to twelve hours a day in one room, in one chair, meditating, reading, studying, or writing, but how can I know why I am here? The only thing that scares me more than searching for my destiny is not meeting it. Perhaps Seth is my destiny. After all, my life is now and will forever be entwined with his. We are like two spokes of a wheel. If he is to move forward, then I need to as well. If he is to be visible, then I must become visible, too.

In Kabbalah there are two levels of wisdom called *Da'at*. The lower Da'at serves as a bridge between the intellect and emotion, idea and action. It is a bridge between wisdom and understanding. The higher Da'at is a place of paradox where the contradictions of left brain and right brain consciousness—two opposite ways of engaging reality—are unified. On the one hand I am totally alone. My son has little language. My parents are long gone. My friends, of course, have families, projects, and preoccupations that come before I do. My passion for my son borders on obsession, which by definition is a lonely place. *Da'at*. On the other hand I am totally supported. My son is loving and caring and since 2003 has found happiness creating art. His joy fills our home. His paintings are his voice. They speak volumes and pulsate with life. Who else could be lucky enough to say these words? My parents' love sustained me. They adored and supported me. They made me who I am. Of course, they are always with me. Although my friends have their own lives, they often choose to be with me. Sometimes they are with me daily. My passion for my son is not mine alone. There is a world of people who believe in him. His mentors show up, contemplate him, and dream about him. He is not just a job.

I am both alone and surrounded by a supportive community. Like the in breath and the out breath. Alone. Community. Both are true. Perhaps paradoxes must be true for any of us to meet our destiny. But

Horizontal Purple Aurora Triptych with Rivers, Lakes, Deciduous, 2007. Oil on canvas, 38 × 30 inches each panel.

I used New Colors. I used Metallic, Gold, Silver, and Bronze. I use Luminescent Colors. I used very thick paint.

01-0

what is my destiny? As I search for it, I manage by ignoring reality and attending to every detail of reality. Both.

LET'S TAKE A RANDOM TIME. As I write this chapter in July 2009, I am living, like everyone else, in the worst economic times since the 1930s. Like everyone else, I have lost money. Like everyone else, I am praying for better times. This is not a good time. We sold eleven paintings in Cayman. We have sold almost no paintings in America for a year. This summer, Seth had a retrospective, a great honor, in Cleveland, and a beautiful well-attended opening in New Jersey. No sales. If I was logical and realistic, we would take a break, slow down. Seth paints many hours a week. Seth never paints alone. All mentors are paid. There is no end to the cost of paint. A few hours less of painting could actually save some money. It would give us time to take long walks, to relax. While it may sound good, cutting Seth's painting hours is not tempting. The life we have is the one where Seth wants to paint. He's happy when he paints. He wants to make people happy. He wants to open at the Time Equities building with his 11-by-26-foot painting of *Manhattan Floating*. Seth paints. I watch. I organize. I fill with joy.

Reality will not stop us. Reduced money. Reduced sales. I ignore it. *Da'at.* I spend two to ten hours a day, every day—including weekends and holidays—taking care of the details of Seth's world and our reality. I love it when Ann takes time away from her family and other obligations to help in any way she can. She is here for only part of the day. The details can drown you. I wake up at 4:00 a.m. and make notes of things to do in the morning. I persevere. I work until I am too tired to think or until my body gives out. My hand starts to burn from writing too long. Seth needs me. So I stop writing, knowing I will soon be back. Reality

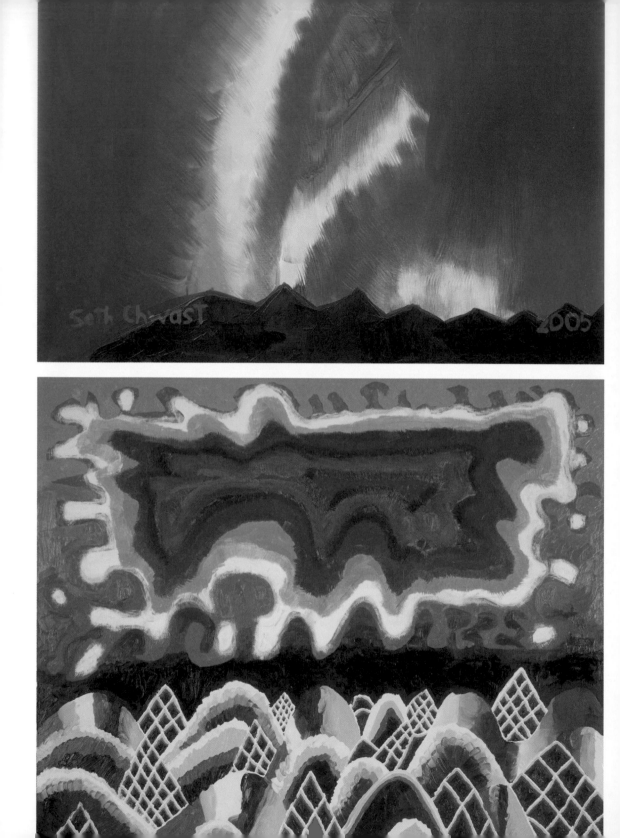

is irrelevant and reality is my world. *Da'at.* I can go forward only by playing both sides.

Who am I? Who is Seth? Lynda Yanks, my good friend, said Seth could be a world icon, the next smiley face. Was she simply telling me what I had to hear to mobilize me, to get me to help Seth move to the next level, or does she know something that I do not? I believe Lynda is a mystic and there are people for whom past, present, and future merge. Mystics have vision and visions. I have had a peek, maybe true, saying Seth will have an impact on the world and it is my job to make this happen. Lynda's vision resonates inside me; it calls to me. *Da'at.* Of course, no one knows the future. If I believe something big will happen and it will give my life meaning, but I am blind and clueless to what that something will be, what should I do? I have loved and been loved by true friends, all of us blind to our destinies, all of us fiercely loyal and determined. Maybe our devotion is all the more touching because we are blind. Isn't that what faith is? A mystic says that Seth is to do something big, and I, the mom, cannot picture or imagine it. So the mystical side and the blind side will go forward together as I search for my destiny.

I LIVE A LIFE OF SERVICE. I was a therapist for thirty-three years. It was not simply a job. I cared about my clients and I looked forward to each hour I spent with them. I was there for them. I stopped working to be able to take care of my father and my son. I became what I called "a therapist with a caseload of two." For me, doing service works. When my father lived with us, I wanted to make every day perfect. Each day, I gave him what he needed. In the beginning of his time with us, we went to the Cleveland College of Jewish Studies four times a week to take classes; we went to concerts, the theater, or dance performances every weekend; and had

OPPOSITE ABOVE:
Peanut Butter Mountains, 2005. Oil on canvas, 20 x 30 inches.

OPPOSITE BELOW:
Waffle Mountains, 2005. Oil on canvas, 52 x 62 inches.

OPPOSITE LEFT: *Rough and Smooth Is an Aurora*, 2006. Oil on canvas, 70 × 84 inches.

I painted Rough and Smooth in 96 hours. I used my smallest brush for the Mountains. I wanted Many Small Shapes and 1 Giant Shape. I used many of Blues, Blue-Greens, Red-Violets, Reds, Oranges, Greens, Yellows, Browns, and Blacks. I like to paint Auroras. I like to paint Many Imaginary Shapes in the Sky that are reflected on Snow-Capped Mountains and on Ice-Covered Rivers and Lakes.

OPPOSITE RIGHT: *Northern Lights with Purple Swirls*, 2005. Oil on canvas, 30 × 40 inches.

Many of Swirls have Names of People. The Pine Trees are in the Foreground. The Mountains are in the Background. Each Swirls is a Person in My Life.

three dinner parties a week and hosted his New York family and friends. Later, he could no longer get dressed or leave the house. It didn't matter. I had rabbis come to the house to give classes twice a week. I invited the community and served lunch. I flew in rabbis David Zeller and Yitzchak Schwartz from Israel for weeklong workshops. Our home was filled with people, stories, life, and music. In the spring and fall my father and I could sit in the garden on and off all day. In the heat of the summer we went out early in the morning and again in the evening. We listened to the music he loved. I kept him dry and clean and told him stories and stayed with him. Sometimes I would look up from helping my dad and remember what it was like to live my life and do what I wanted when I wanted. But for me that was a shadow of a life. It paled beside the life of giving life, of giving loved ones what they need or want, of bringing them joy, whether they are like Seth and can't fend for themselves or like my dad in his last year, month, week, or day. To me, that is truly living.

Kabbalah teaches us to never give up. If the knife is against your throat, never give up. From the time Seth was diagnosed, I was driven by my need for him to have a great life. I wanted for my son what everyone wants for their children. We would not be obstructed by a problem—even if that problem was autism. Yes, for ten years I hoped he would somehow come out of his autism and we did every therapy possible. Then I searched for what would make him happy, what would fill him with passion, what would bring him into the world. While I searched, we played lots of Nintendo and took lots of roller coaster trips. I never gave up.

When I found that Seth could paint, I was not thinking of him selling art, supporting himself, or being in museums. I had never heard of "Outsider Art." I was a mom working with my son to create a life. It was the summer of 2003, and I had filed for divorce in April. I wanted to start a new life filled with joy, color, music, and people. I had a new friend who was a party planner so I had a series of parties. Each one had a theme—a Turkish party, a Hungarian party, a pie party, a Klezmer party, a "come-in-your-robe" party (because my dad could now wear only robes). For every party Seth made a painting. The paintings were magnificent. Where would they lead? I didn't know. I didn't care. I wanted a perfect day for my dad and my son, whatever day it was. Two of Seth's mentors were art therapists. Hospice sent an art therapist to work with Seth and his Poppy. Was the art therapy? Of course. Art pulled Seth into communication, into community, into finally being visible. Is Seth an artist? Left alone he has never picked up a brush. He never initiates. That may be the autism. Give him a mentor and he wears them out. He needs two a day. He leaves them inspired by his focus and his perseverance. Seth loves color. When he worked on one of his paintings of the aurora borealis, he said he wanted seventeen blues, nineteen greens, and eleven reds. Then he mixed seventeen blues, each one a combination of two, three, four, or five tubes of different blue paints. He kept mixing and looking until he had his seventeen blues, certain of what he wanted.

We, Seth and I, as a team have won. We did it. Seth gets up every morning happy and excited. He names his mentors and tells me what he will be working on first. He sings and hums and jumps up and down and claps. This is all before he starts to paint and really gets happy. We found a full-time therapy that keeps Seth focused, growing, and in a state of bliss. His art is his therapy. His art is a lifeline. His art is his life. I am still a mom, working to give my son what he needs. Perhaps my destiny is to live a life of service. Perhaps living a life of service will burn away everything unessential, and whatever is left will be the real me—the me that I've been searching for.

In Kabbalah we learn to see with G-d's eyes. We do not see the person standing before us with all their warts and imperfections. We see them as the best they can be, as the person that, in the end, they will be revealed to be. This is a gift beyond measure. To be seen that way creates us, focuses us, helps us manifest as our best. To see others that way turns us into midwives, helps us birth and transform loved ones.

My father, Milton J. Newmark, saw me. He looked at me with such love that I sometimes had to lower my eyes. The intensity in them was like looking at the sun. By the end, I was his moon and his stars, his day and his night, his all. He knew what I did for him. He called our home his five-star hotel. He knew what I did for Seth. Before we discovered painting, he listened for hours as I brainstormed and tried every way I could think of to help Seth. After 2003 my dad fully embraced Seth's art and he was totally supportive and devoted, doing everything he could to propel us forward. I could tell my father anything and he listened and believed as I talked about my spiritual experiences—my moments of grace so profound that it was difficult to speak of them. He heard what I said and honored me and my experiences. He believed me and he believed in me. He believed in Seth. I lost my dad inch by inch to stroke after stroke. In six years he went from a cane to a walker to a wheelchair to needing a man to help him stand, pivot, and transfer from his wheelchair to his lift chair. He was the most eloquent of men but he lost his voice and he could only whisper. After the strokes he lost his words. He lost everything but his immense mind and his ability to love. He was as dear to me as he had ever been. When he looked at me, he knew he was adored and admired, trusted, and needed.

My father and I both saw Seth. Seth knows this. I call Seth "Angel of G-d." I always did. He is pure and sweet and good and smart and kind. Seth has been adored since he was born. Love is catching. My parents loved me. I love my son. I love my friends. When I love, I see others as perfect, as who they truly are and who they will be. It is a gift. I cannot yet turn those eyes on myself. Now that my father is gone, who will see me? Seth sees me. Seth stares at me and I tell him his eyes are like jewels.

He tells me roller coaster facts and I hear the metaphors of his life and I listen. He watches me watching him, and the intensity of being seen transforms both of us again and again. How do we become the best we can be? How do we find out who we truly are? How do we tolerate the ambiguity and the uncharted territory? Support, doing service, being seen, loving, and being loved all help. We also need determination, perseverance, and the ability to tolerate rejection and failure. Whenever I think it's too hard, too overwhelming, too complicated, and I simply can't do it, I remember that there is me and there is Seth and one of us has to do it. So I go forward. That is what Kabbalah calls "the power of no choice." If I don't do it, who will?

One Big Vertical Aurora with 2 Pine Trees, Mountains, 2007. Oil on canvas, 60 × 36 inches.

Seth Chwast

02-16-07

CHAPTER 7

Portrait Of the Artist

As a three-year-old, Seth ate only white and yellow food: cottage cheese, Muenster cheese, apples, bananas, bread, applesauce, Cheerios, and pancakes. He was passionate about ice cream. He would climb up the refrigerator, sit on top, reach down, open the freezer, and reach in for ice cream. Sometimes he would open the refrigerator door and climb up the shelves, then open the freezer door and eat ice cream while sitting on the refrigerator shelf.

Seth was almost four years old when we attempted potty training. We put him on the pot, gave him a book to keep him there, and found out he could read. That was the good news. Accidents were the bad news. One day Seth's dad and our friend Teena took Seth to the zoo. Seth was riding on his dad's head when he had an accident. It was quite a mess. Suffice it to say, there were lots of accidents. But there was good news, too. For one M&M he would take his pants down, pee, flush, and pull his pants up. For one M&M! What a deal! But the accidents continued. I don't even remember when they stopped. Certainly not by age six and maybe not even by age eight.

We had hard times, lots of them. And in the midst, there were great stories. As I mentioned before, Seth is musically gifted. When I sang him lullabies at eighteen months, he would cover my mouth because I was off-key! At age two he fell in love with Brahms's violin concerto. He listened to it for hours. We had tapes of it for him to listen to wherever he went. There was one at music therapy, one at language therapy, and one at his special preschool. He loved that music. Seth was three when he first heard Sibelius's powerful Symphony no. 1 in E Minor. He ran screaming from the room.

Silver Fantasy Pegasus #4 with Man in the Sky, 2007. Oil on canvas, 48 × 36 inches.

An Unexpected Life

By the time he was eight, you could bring Seth into a room with someone playing piano, turn his head or cover his eyes so he couldn't see the keyboard, and ask him to name the specific chord that was being played. He would say "Augmented G7" or "Diminished A5." He never missed. Franklin Cohen, principal clarinetist in the Cleveland Symphony Orchestra, lives two doors down. He came over to check out Seth's musical ability. He played a few chords on the piano and Seth named them. Then he hit three keys at once that were not a chord and Seth named the three notes. He hit four keys at once for an instant and Seth named them. I ventured, "I think he has perfect pitch." Franklin asked, "Is Seth composing yet?" He was absolutely serious. As a matter of fact, Seth had composed two songs but I hadn't paid much attention to them. Although music was important to us and we enjoyed the symphony and listened to music at home, it wasn't the center of our life. When I look back on what Franklin said, it makes me think. Life is random and interesting. If Seth had been Franklin's son, he might have been a musical prodigy. Instead, Seth became an artist.

When he was little, we thought Seth loved going to the zoo to see the animals. It was clear from the look on his face that he loved the zoo tram and the lemonade. But I began to realize that the animals did not excite or even interest him. He never looked at them or reached out to pet them. He didn't seem to even notice the elephants! For him the petting zoo was a playground. The incubator was a toy to be manipulated, rather than the home of future chicks. He didn't pay attention to the goats: The goat pen was something to climb up on. He was oblivious to the ducks. Finally, it hit me. I had always thought his problems were auditory, because he didn't talk. But the way he behaved at the zoo helped me realize that Seth's problems were also visual and attentive. The way he took in the world must have been beyond anything I could even imagine.

The Red Gray Fantasy Horse, 2007. Acrylic on canvas, 36 × 18 inches.

The Portrait of Horse. The Horse has Whole Face. I am excited. The Horse Feels proud and Thrilled. This Painting was very hard to Do.

FOR MOST OF SETH's childhood I was frantic, confused, weepy, and in over my head. But in the midst of all this I have wonderful memories. Seth is three. On a warm summer night, with a sky filled with stars, Seth comes outside with me when I take out the garbage. Seth's little toy trampoline is on the lawn and as we go by it, Seth climbs up and starts to jump. One part of me reflexively wants to object. It's 10:00 p.m., time for bed. Another part of me stares in wonder. Maybe Seth's right. Maybe it's a great idea. Maybe it's a perfect time for jumping on a trampoline. It is a warm, beautiful night and there is no real reason to go to sleep at this exact moment. He is laughing and filled with joy. I sit down. The tension of the day, the week, the whole autistic year starts to drain from my body. Maybe his reality is better than my reality. I respect Seth. I don't feel smarter or more powerful or more right. I can learn from him. And I do.

When Seth was three he loved it when I slid under the living room coffee table on my back. Once I was under there we had a giant body-sized game of peekaboo. I have no idea how the game first began. He loved to see me go under, slowly disappear, and slowly reappear. It's not exactly my idea of fun, but he laughed and giggled and shrieked with joy so I did it again. And again. And again. He was so happy. Fortunately, rather than let my idea of fun rule, I let Seth vote. We do what fills him with joy. The world said Seth was autistic. My heart told me he was joyful, creative, and fun-loving. For an autistic child who supposedly couldn't relate, Seth adored me. He could relate to me. He was simply different from other people and connected in his own way.

When we gave Seth gifts, like most toddlers, he loved the paper bags they came in. I'd pick a beautiful, brightly colored Brio toy. Did he like the toy? Maybe. But the paper bag! That caused joy. If he preferred a paper bag to a Brio toy, he'd play with the bag for as long as it intrigued him.

One day, when he was around five years old, Seth's language therapist gave him an ink pad and a stamp in the shape of a triangle. Seth stamped a few triangles. Then he stamped out a star. Next, he seemed to be stamping a random design. When he was done, in the center of the dark triangles, in the negative space, was a perfect white star—something I could not have done! His language therapist said, "A lot of graduate level art students would have trouble doing that so easily."

If I had listened carefully with my heart or with a sense of the sky is the limit, I might have heard his language therapist telling me that Seth had an amazing visual gift. But I was so determined that he gain language that I couldn't see anything beyond that goal. All of our energy was focused like a laser on that one objective. If I could have thought outside the box for a minute, I might have considered his artistic gift to be a better ability than language. I wasn't yet ready for the message. However, if someone said, "Would you like your son to speak or be Picasso," what would you say?

Usually those are the questions and conundrums of fairy tales. *So, Little Mermaid, would you rather sing (your greatest gift), or walk and gain love (one of the world's greatest gifts)?* When it comes down to it, we are not presented with such choices. Yet fairy tales and their dilemmas touch something archetypal, something real for all of us. I wanted Seth to be normal. Desperately. And, in a bizarre way, at the same time, he seemed fine the way he was. Actually, he seemed more magical than fine. I never saw Seth as a victim who would or would not be victorious over his challenge. I never felt pity or wanted anyone else's pity. His essence was so powerful. He was simply his own person, whole in who he was. In the end, I had to make a choice for myself about how I would work with Seth and how I viewed his autism. I was the one who asked myself unanswerable questions.

Seth has always been certain of what makes him happy. If he was in bliss and the world called him autistic, did he have a problem?

Six Self Studies, 2005. Acrylic on canvas, 70 × 84 inches.

TOP ROW, LEFT TO RIGHT: [Pthalo Blue] Happy. I am astonished. 07/28/05; [Green Ochre] Excited. I Feel Thrilled, 07/29/05; [Emerald Green] I Feel relaxed, 07/29/05.

BOTTOM ROW, LEFT TO RIGHT: [Ultramarine Blue] I feel Proud. Sad. 07/30/05; [Gray] I feel independent. Confused. 07/30/05; [Rose] I feel concerned. Worried. 08/04/05; I feel relaxed—I finished hair. 08/05/05.

Did I? In our house, particularly in front of a canvas with a brush in his hand, Seth did not have a problem; we did not have a problem. Step outside, interface with reality, we had a catastrophe. From the inside, it was atypical and bizarre and sort of wonderful. On the outside, it was atypical and bizarre and upsetting.

Let's look at a typical day in the life of Seth Chwast. If Seth is going to paint mid-morning, he has to get up at least a couple of hours before then. But he has no sense of time, so it is up to me or me and Ann to rouse him from bed and keep him on track as he gets ready for the day. He likes a bath in the morning, and as I mentioned before, when I say bath, I mean a long, long bath. Is this good or bad? Wouldn't you like to float in bubbles for an hour, ignoring reality? I urge him to finish: "Seth, quick as a bunny! Seth, you have to paint in one hour and you still have to eat breakfast!"

Seth replies, "Quick as a bunny . . . Quick as a mouse . . . Quick as a flying saucer . . . Emergency, 911." He throws out one of these phrases every five minutes. But what does he do? He floats. He adds more hot water. He doesn't move for about an hour. Is this a problem? Or is it the essence of the good life?

Seth likes to wear sweatpants and a T-shirt. They are his favorite clothes. If he is not busy painting, he changes his T-shirts frequently. It seems that every time I see him, he has on a new shirt. One day there were eighteen shirts down the laundry shoot. I folded them and put them back on his shelf. Is this a problem? Maybe he loves going from purple to red to teal. Maybe you and I would feel a lot better if we changed clothing eighteen times a day. Maybe it is more comfortable for him to change or he simply likes the variety. Maybe it's just fine; different, but fine.

Seth calls only one phone number, ever. He calls Cedar Point, his favorite roller coaster park, about once a day. At first this startled me. I'd walk in and see him on the phone, sharing roller coaster facts with great animation. I'd take the phone, introduce myself, and explain that Seth was autistic. And the person on the other end of the line would say, "Oh, it's okay. We know Seth. He calls us all the time." I know that if there was a fire, Seth would not think to call 911. I know he has never made a practical phone call in his life. But he wants to call Cedar Point. He enjoys it. And they enjoy him. Maybe this is okay. Maybe it's more than fine.

Have you ever been hurt or betrayed by someone you love? Don't all shout at once! None of us enjoys random slights, hurts, or attacks. It is hard for me when I trust and love someone, believe in them, and then they turn on me. I also hate it when they rewrite events and then deeply believe their version. It's happened to me; it's happened to you. Guess what? Seth is unable to do this. He can't lie or distort or figure out any part of that game. One day when he was little and wasn't supposed to eat anything before dinner, I walked into the kitchen and found him eating cookies. I said, "Oh, Seth, how many cookies did you eat?" I didn't really expect an answer. In the same situation, most people, including myself, might say "One" to mitigate the crime. Seth said "Seven." After all the times that people have betrayed me, dropped me, confused me, blamed me, or insisted that I had it all wrong, Seth heals me. He heals me by never lying, distorting, misremembering; he heals me by being authentic, by not telling me black is white, by not telling me he said A but really meant B and I should have understood that. He heals me just by being who he is.

Most people try to make the world work to their advantage. That is not part of Seth's makeup. He does what he does without keeping to a timetable or to fulfill anyone else's expectations. He can take eleven hours to paint a 70-by-84-inch canvas, but he once spent ninety-six hours on another canvas of identical size. He might use a roller to make huge strokes, or a tiny brush for miniscule strokes. He is outside the world of time management or efficiency. He will make thick swirls of oil paint in his trees and paint over them. He doesn't do this for the texture; he could create texture in other ways. He just wants to know the hidden swirls are there, under what the eye can see. One time he drew mountains out of geometric shapes—hearts, diamonds, trapezoids, octagons. They were so beautiful. I was certain he'd make each shape a different color. Instead, he obliterated them. He wanted them there and then he covered them. He wanted the joy of knowing they were there. He paints for himself, and for the pleasure of it. I find this purity to be healing. Each painting removes another layer of the pain of living.

The Boy Who Turned into a Tree, 2008. Acrylic on canvas, 60 × 60 inches.

The New York City is in the Background. Trees are growing from the Buildings. The Windows are stained glass. The Glass Windows have colors. The Clouds are Different Hues of Green. The Boy is a self-study. The Boy will turn into a Tree. The Boy feels glad. I paint a lot of leaves. I am proud of this painting.

Everything Seth does is pure. He has no idea of how he affects people. By twenty-five, Seth started composing at music therapy. I asked his music therapist Lori Smith if he is talented. "These are not simple compositions. He composes a half hour a week. If he spent forty hours a week on music, who knows what he could do? He has perfect pitch. He can compose without checking anything. He hears it in his head. I had to explain arranging. The composing simply pours out of him. He does it without effort." Seth composes like he paints. Intensely focused, only if a mentor is there, but there may be no limit to his ability and he is filled with joy as beauty flows out from him.

I once heard that the composer Rossini said he wrote music the way apples fell off trees. It was that simple, easy, and natural for him. This is how Seth paints. Once, Seth had painted for most of the day and finally went to bed around 10:30. At 12:30 I heard him crowing with joy. I ran to his room to find him in bed, grinning and laughing. He was too excited to sleep. I stayed with him for an hour, while he named his paintings over and over.

I'm so glad my dad lived to see Seth's joy in painting. During the last months of my dad's life, Seth and his mentors would carry huge canvases of newly finished paintings into my dad's bedroom. He was so thrilled and excited. Seth would jump and clap. I'd run and get my camera. Those were peak experiences for all of us.

Each group of new paintings is seen by his photographer, his archivist, and his mentors, professional people who fill with excitement as Seth continues to expand his horizons. For Seth, his art brings him into community, his openings are his life events. Art pulls him into language and into the web of life. His art is his way of communicating. For us, his art is hope. To walk into a room filled with Seth's paintings is to feel joy—people tell me they feel happy, calm, and exhilarated. Reality fades a bit. Some tension drains away. They get caught in a detail and then are overwhelmed by the size, the color, his vision. They smile. They laugh. They feel good. The more openings Seth has, the more confident he becomes. His art is becoming more original, more unique. He is finding his voice. Each day it grows stronger and more vibrant.

I'm starting to understand that Seth is no longer simply my son. He is in the world, of the world, and starting to belong to the world.

A Cleveland Institute of Art student, Matt, came into our lives in January 2008 as a mentor. He is a realist painter. His paintings look like photographs. We scheduled his first visit for a Saturday, from noon to

five. He stayed until seven and returned on Sunday from noon to seven. Seth was so excited he could not contain himself. He kept jumping up and down. Seth did the most amazing bird painting, *2 Waved Albatross Heads.* He kept saying, "More, Matt." Matt kept saying, "This is my dream job." By Sunday night, Matt said, "Seth is where I thought he would be in two months. I cannot believe how fast he learns, how good he is." We stared at the birds. They look like real birds. Where did they come from? I watched Seth paint them. He did every stroke. And the birds are plump, fat, and alive. But Seth is the fantasy man. He loves flat, two-dimensional figures. Where would this lead?

In 2003, Seth wanted to do a painting of an elephant. We went to the library and took out elephant books. He picked an Indian elephant in

2 Waved Albatross Heads, diptych, 2008. Oil on canvas, 18 × 24 each panel.

The Waved Albatross is courting. My Friend Daniel Fitter Angermeyer took a photograph of these Birds. I saw Waved Albatross flying in The Sky and sitting on the Ground in the Galapagos Islands. These Birds have Hues of Pinks, Yellow, Tans, Oranges, Whites, Creams, Browns, Violets, and Black. The Grass has Different Hues of Greens. The Grass has blades of different shapes. The Grass has angles. The Birds like each other. I like the Birds. It is a real painting. It is not a fantasy painting. I feel glad. The Birds feel happy and excited.

full dress for a festival. He made a drawing in pencil in his sketchbook. It was an almost perfect copy, although his elephant was a bit thinner, a bit more expressive. It was splendid. His first art mentor Donna took Seth and his sketchbook to the Cleveland Museum of Natural History. He stood there in front of the elephant and drew a front view of its head, the trunk in air. His elephant had large human eyes with eyelashes. This was the elephant he would paint, rather than the beautiful Indian elephant. Then I understood. Any art student could copy an illustration, but no one else could make Seth's unique fantasy elephant. Since the beginning with Donna, Seth painted these inner visions. She never let him copy, as she felt it was too easy, too tempting, and would not help Seth find his voice. Now, in walked Matt the realist, asking Seth to look at photos and to copy.

Before Matt started to mentor Seth, I explained to him how the painting process with Seth had to work. No one but Seth could touch his canvas. It must be 100 percent Seth. As Seth worked on the bird painting, Matt said "Hold out your hand, palm down. The light is on the top. The top of your hand is so light. Look at it. Look at your palm. It is so dark. There is no light. The bottom of the bird is in the shadow. It must be your darkest color. Pick a dark color." "Where do you want highlight? Where is the sun?" At the end there was a realistic painting of waved albatross. Is it Seth? Is it an Indian elephant? Was Seth being reduced to being a copyist? What is a realist and what is a copyist? I wanted Seth to find his voice. Matt wanted him to learn basic skills. I called Kip, Seth's mentor in Brooklyn. Kip said, "It's fine. It's art school. Nothing will stop Seth. Do not worry." I usually let Seth's mentors do what they wish, but I made a request of Matt. Could Matt merge his desire for Seth to increase his skills with my desire for Seth to find his voice? Matt assured me that he and Seth will go that way. I am shocked by how good Seth is as a baby realist. I am in awe watching every painting.

When we were getting ready for the March 2008 Galapagos opening, Seth was painting with Donna during the week and with Matt on weekends. He was also sculpting with Noah, a Cleveland Institute of Art graduate, three mornings a week. Seth finished sculpting three horses, and then moved to five sea lions and three giant tortoises. These are baked white clay painted teal, lavender, purple, salmon, navy, and the multitude of colors that Seth so loves. He started a series of Galapagos birds, oil on canvas, 24 by 18 inches, small enough to carry with us. These include the 2 *Waved Albatross* that he did with Matt as his mentor. Those birds made me see that Seth is a better painter than I understood. If I had not been there the entire fourteen hours that he painted the albatross, I would've said, "No way. Seth did not, Seth could not do that." I am not saying they are his best. They are "realistic." People might prefer fantasy. Seth may prefer fantasy. He may do realistic birds in fantasy colors. He may never do anything like them again. But Seth did the unpredictable. He painted beyond and outside of his range, which may mean that he could truly be a man with unknown boundaries, unknown limits. I feel honored to have watched this unfold.

Here is an example of a day in my life with Seth—say March 3, 2008—Seth was asked to be the artist for a $500-a-plate benefit for Autism Speaks at the Rock and Roll Hall of Fame and Museum. For that event, Seth wanted to paint Elton John's *Rocket Man*. I felt frantic. I couldn't interrupt Seth's work for the Galapagos opening. Seth had nine more sea lion paintings that had been started and needed to be finished with Matt. Seth and Donna were working nonstop on fish and Galapagos sea turtles. So, Noah agreed to switch to painting. He and Seth opened the computer and printed out images from *The Rocketeer* (the 1991 movie), in which the masked hero flew in the air with a rocket pack strapped on, as well as images of the moon and the earth, and explosions in the sky. Seth percolated these images to start his *Rocket Man*.

I left a message for Marni Deutch, producer of Gallery HD—a high-definition TV channel (now closed)—about the DVD they were considering making of Seth. I sent *Lonesome George*, Seth's sculpture of a specific giant tortoise in the Galapagos, and his painting *The Green Sea Lion on Violet*, off to Larry Kasperek, the tech guy who maintains Seth's database for his website, and his partner, Al Fuchs, the photographer who is archiving Seth's work. I arranged for them to receive those works and to send back a batch of paintings and sculptures that had already been photographed and archived. We got an e-mail from Marni and she wanted to know our travel schedule. Me too!! Could they film Seth in his home? Could they interview his first art teacher? Has he had exhibitions? It seems the film went from a maybe to a highly likely. I answered and told her that I would send her a press kit (which needed to be updated).

I felt almost dizzy with swirling potential. Seth seemed unstoppable.

SETH IS EVERYTHING I WANT TO BE. He is authentic. Think of someone like the Dalai Lama or Mother Teresa, not someone who merely loves, but someone who is love, someone whose essence is love. That is Seth. Picture a Zen kind of guy. When he eats, he eats with total concentration and joy. At the end, quickly licking the tip of each of his ten fingers, he will be humming in bliss. He is free of greed, jealousy, envy, resentment, or anger. His primary emotional state is, *I feel happy; I feel excited.* If something is wrong, he says, "I feel anxious. I feel nervous. I feel sad." He tells you exactly how he feels and trusts you will help him. Soon enough he is humming again. Seth is highly social in his own way. It is not an option in his mind to think that somebody might not like him. His music therapist, Lori, gave him lists of topics to help him start conversations. They are rote but he really is interested. He will ask how old you are, and then tell you the year you were born. Where do you live? What is your favorite vacation? How many children do you have? What are their names? How many friends do you have? We met the curator of a hospital gallery to present Seth's work. She accepted his art and scheduled the dates. That was their only contact. Almost a year later, at the opening of his exhibition, Seth recognized her, named her children, and told her how old they were. She was charmed. I was amazed.

Rocket Man, 2008. Oil on canvas, 18 × 24 inches.

The Rocket Man is for Elton John. The Rocket Man has Different Tones of Grays, Silvers, and Blacks. The Rocket Man's Fire has Different Hues of Oranges, Tangerines, Marmalades, Apricots, Peaches, Reds, Yellows, Mangoes, Papayas, and Guavas. The Implosion has Hues of Blues, Purples, and Grays. The shape of Implosion has burst. The Sky is Black. The Sky has many different Shaped Clouds of different colors. The Sky has many Planets. The Pluto was kicked out. I feel sad about Pluto.

In June 2007, when Perry introduced Seth to Kip, this was the beginning of Seth traveling in and out of New York, moving into a larger world. Traveling with Seth is never what I would call easy. For each trip, I had to send Seth with a Cleveland artist mentor who could help Seth feel secure and help Kip pick up Seth's rhythm. I went. Ann Kocks went. It takes a village . . . but we have found a way to make it work.

Our dear friend Francis Greenburger helped us bring Seth further into the world by introducing him to the admissions committee of the Art Omi International Artists Residency in August 2007. As I mentioned earlier, this resulted in a three-week residency in Ghent in July 2008. Because Seth has no sense of physical danger, someone must be with him 24/7. This is a major challenge, especially when he travels. The idea of going to Ghent was both exciting and intimidating. It took months of planning, and much anxiety on my part, to get us ready to go. But we did it. On big trips there are tag teams of people who are responsible for his art and his person. When he went to Art Omi, Kip went as his mentor. I stayed for the whole time. Seth had never been away from home for so long. It was an opportunity that I never thought could happen in our lives. I could not say no, and I was overwhelmed at having said yes.

Much of my concern was fueled by other people's inability to understand just how vulnerable Seth was. For example, one day Seth, Ann, and I were at the Museum of Modern Art (MoMA) in New York with an artist mentor, a young female university student. Seth wanted to tour around with this "same age" friend and she agreed that she would watch him. When she stopped to take photographs with her cell phone, Seth wandered off. Ann saw it happen, grabbed Seth, and explained to the young woman that if she was with Seth, she had to be totally responsible for him. No problem. Minutes later, the same thing happened again. Now we knew that this young woman could not watch Seth. If Seth wandered off, he would have no way to find us. After working with

Seth for almost a year, this young woman could not understand the level of responsibility that she had when she was with him. "He seems fine," she said. So Seth and I often travel with Ann and an artist mentor, if we need one. This is the baseline requirement.

Any travel or bringing Seth into a situation near food requires the same heightened awareness. Left alone at a table, he will dab his pinky into the butter (dairy, which he cannot metabolize) and lick his finger! In a grocery store, he will dart ahead and eat all of the cheese and cracker samples (dairy again, and wheat, also verboten) before I can catch up and grab him. I literally have to hold him back when we enter.

MoMA—Museum of Modern Art in Manhattan, New York, 2007. Acrylic on wood, 12 × 12 inches.

149

Watching Seth requires vigilance and stamina. Seth, who is six feet tall, runs up to strangers and asks, in rapid succession, "How old are you? Where do you live? What is your e-mail? What is your favorite vacation?" In an airport this could happen twenty times in one hour. At every moment, while we are in public, someone has to help Seth and have no other distractions or responsibility.

Let's look at a few other random days, back in the beginning of Seth's journey. On October 9, 2007, I took Seth's dictation as he named his nine clay horses, including *Blue Fantasy Horse's Head with Details of Long Orange Mane, Red Lips, Blue Nostrils, Yellow Eyes with Orange Iris + Dark Blue Ears*. He dictated that one as he floated in the tub! I love it. Then I measured each horse, put the list in chronological order, sent it to Larry to put in the database, and called Al to get it photographed. I called three artists about Seth's painting schedule and Noah about whether to bake the last clay horse. I spoke to Joan Perch, who was our agent at the time. Can she pick up the clay horses from the photographer and bring them to the exhibition? Can we get T-shirts with photo transfers of Seth's frogs for the opening? Last week we spent three hours tweaking the CD for his press kit. We now go over the next layer of details. That is just the morning.

In late October 2007, we got a phone call from Amanda Marshall of the *Today* show. She wanted to know how Seth was doing, and what happened after they left. We told her about Seth's mentor in New York and the Art Omi residency. On November 2, Amanda called back. They wanted to film Seth again, painting in Brooklyn in December,

Blue Fantasy Horse Head with Details of Long Orange Mane, Red Lips, Blue Nostrils, Yellow Eyes with Orange Iris + Dark Blue Ears, 2007. White oven-baked clay with acrylic paint, 5 × 8 × approximately 5 inches.

and show it on New Year's Day! He would be the story of the year, their favorite story of 2007. Seth could not stop jumping and laughing. He was thrilled.

There was so much excitement. We bought tickets for Seth to see Cirque du Soleil, the Rockettes Christmas Show, and *Xanadu*. We would go to Perry's holiday party, to MoMA, and to the American Museum of Folk Art. It was the kind of energy my mother adored. It made me feel close to her. In the midst of all the planning and physical realities, I started to feel that my whole life was shifting into beauty, unlimited potential, and new realities. Back then, I did not know it, but I was right. Our world burst into everything I had hoped for and more. There was no way to anticipate the world's reaction to Seth's art and his story.

There is no single way to capture the essence of Seth. He is fire always consuming new experiences, always needing someone to stoke his flame. He is a roller coaster, slowly chugging along step-by-step, picking up energy, and then accelerating into the wildest plunge over and over and over. Seth is also a thin sheet of ice over a river. The river is there and flowing but the ice needs to be broken a bit for the river's power to come through. Seth is Pinocchio; loved by his family but never considered a contender by the outside world, he turned into a real boy. He is a man who by age twenty-eight has been on the *Today* show twice and laughs with joy as his shows open in Galapagos and the National Gallery of the Cayman Islands. He is Botticelli's Venus on the half-shell, emerging full-formed from the sea foam, living twenty years without picking up a crayon, a pencil, or a paintbrush, taking a four-day art class, and three months later painting *Hungarian Horse and Peacock*, a work of such power and beauty as to defy description. Can he be fire and a roller coaster and a river and Pinocchio and Venus all at once? Yes, and more. He is an icon of hope. He brings joy. His story is the way "Never give up" walks the earth.

Today I am ready to talk to the world about autism. I couldn't use the word for years because I didn't want Seth to be pigeon-holed or limited. I didn't want anyone to dismiss him or assume that he was not capable. I couldn't use the word until I was certain that he would never be limited by it. Seth is not a victim who is victorious. He is a singular person who is victorious. He is his own person. He is whole in who he is. Seth is in the right place at the right time with the right stuff. I never said, "He can't do that." I always said, "Seth, do you want to do that?" I suffered. Any mom of an autistic person has their hands full. If you have an autistic child, what you have suffered, I may have suffered. After the diagnosis, I wept for the next three years. I was beyond the pale. I thought my pain would split the earth. Now Seth is twenty-eight. I don't see our life filled with sorrow, but with more riches than I could have imagined.

Seth is an artist and he has a career because he has talent and because I never accepted any limits. We live a life with no limits. We were guided by Seth's interests. I never assumed anything was beyond him. I went to Berkeley for graduate school with a guy in a wheelchair, a quadriplegic, who took notes with a pencil attached to his head. I opened door after door for Seth. I did everything I could to give him a fair chance to find his passion. I never assumed that he'd just sit around in a room. Since 2003, I have spent two to eight hours a day most days on the world of Seth's art. Sometimes he wants to paint day and night. Sometimes he will take a week off or sculpt but not paint. It's so important to let him direct his life. Seth is an artist with a public presence who competes both in the world of Outsider Art and with regular artists because he has the talent and because I work every day to create a sacred space in which he can function.

Who is Seth? On May 13, 2008, Marni and two assistants from Gallery HD flew in to meet us. They filmed for nine hours a day for two days. A friend who was interviewed said she was humbled by Seth. I was so moved, I do not remember the rest of what she said. An hour later, Donna, who missed the first interview, was filmed saying that *she* was humbled by Seth.

Who is Seth? Let me tell you right now, loud and clear: Seth is an artist who is autistic. He is not an autistic artist. Seth is not his autism. He is not defined by his autism. Seth is an artist. He is funny, kind, focused, passionate, handsome, autistic, musical, and a little outside of time and space in the real world. I struggle not to let others limit him. I struggle more not to let myself limit him. I yearn for him to be the best he can be and for him to find every single talent and power inside him.

Hungarian Horse and Peacock, 2003. Oil on canvas, 52 × 62 inches.

A) The Hungarian Horse and Peacock has king. The crown is gold. The peacock has many colors of feathers. The horse has design of mosaic. I feel enthusiastic! The painting feels calm. B) I was 20 yrs. old in 2003. I made a painting of my Birthday Cake. I was 21 yrs. old. The Hungarian Horse has King has Gold Crown. The Hungarian Peacock has Feathers. Many Colors are grow Your brain.

CHAPTER 8

Dreams II

Lots of people can paint. There are many great artists in the world who have immeasurable talent. Seth's power is that he is Seth. He happens to be autistic and he creates breathtaking art. The shock comes from the juxtaposition, the contrast, and the irony. Beauty, power, color, and creativity pour out of him.

When Seth was nine, we went to Disney World. A guard opened a separate car on the monorail, let only us in, and said, "You'll be more comfortable if you're by yourself." I was speechless. She went on to say that she had an autistic twelve-year-old. I wept—both from her kindness and because she instantly knew that Seth was autistic. At that time I was still hoping he was not autistic, but that if he was no one could tell.

Now we have come full circle. The moms of autistic children all know within seconds, even if they don't speak English, that Seth is like their child. It's the idea of Seth creating the art that fills them with joy and hope.

I thought we would travel to expose Seth to the world's color and beauty and to give him a chance to transform his art. That was my motivation. I didn't know it would provide a way for him not only to see the world, but to meet its people! I never dreamed that the T-shirts with photo transfers of his art would give him his first acceptable way to start a conversation. There were also people who saw the shirts, loved the art, and reached out to Seth. They came up to talk, took his card, and asked about his paintings. Seth traveled to Galapagos with five small prints, wanting them to go out into the world. Four are now in Ecuador and one is in Switzerland, all with people who love his art.

Rockets in Space, detail from *Manhattan Floating*, 2010. Acrylic on canvas, 64 × 48 inches.

Seth now paints almost daily. We balance it with travel so it's a lot of painting when he is home and then long breaks. I would settle for this. It seems like enough. Sometimes it seems like too much. But what if this is just the tip of the iceberg? Seth says, "Malta." Seth says, "Greenland." Seth says, "Curaçao." Now I know the drill. If Seth says, "Malta," we have to research nonprofits and curators, go to Malta, meet directors and curators, absorb the colors and light of Malta, take photos, go home, paint images of Malta, and return for an opening. Every destination turns into two trips and three months of painting. Seth can dream a bit faster than I can organize. If I'm not fast enough, Seth goes forward without me. Seth wants Italy. He painted three Italian landscapes, including *Tuscany Landscape #2*, while I was still working on Curaçao.

Seth said, "Oprah," "Sir Elton John," and "Bob Dylan, Big Bird, and Sid Caesar." He wanted to create paintings for these celebrities. The *Rocket Man* paintings for Sir Elton John included all the planets. He

RIGHT: *Tuscany Landscape #2*, 2009. Oil on canvas, 18 × 24 inches.

The Sky and Clouds have Different Hues of Peaches, Carrots, Orange Peppers, Cantaloupes, Oranges, Orange Creamsicles, Orange Cake Frostings, Orangeades, Orange Drinks, Orange Pops, Dark Oranges and Light Oranges. The Mountains and Hills have Different Hues of Sages, Ice Greens, Green-Grays, Teals, Turquoises, Cobalt Turquoises, Dark Greens, Grays, and Dark Teals. The Trees have Different Hues of Dark Greens and the Bushes have Different Hues of Dark Teals. The House has Different Hues of Dark Teals. The House includes the Roof and the Window. I want to have an Art Show in Italy.

could easily do a whole series of *Rocket Man* paintings. What if one of these people commissions a painting from Seth and it turns out that they love elephants or clowns or Venice? I think I know the answer to that one. He will immerse himself into whatever place or animal or person he needs to paint and then create art that is uniquely Seth.

Seth picks the subjects he will paint for each theme. When I asked, "Do you want to paint Galapagos?" He said, "Yes." "What will you paint?" I asked. "Giant tortoises, sea lions, birds." But no matter what he is painting, he comes to his canvas with vision and joy.

I had a house full of art before Seth started to paint. I have taken down piece after piece and replaced them with Seth's work. I don't know if Seth's art is technically better than art by other artists. All I know is that I love to have his paintings in my home, and when others see them they think they are wonderful, too. I feel privileged to be surrounded by so much color and joy. I never could have imagined Seth creating art, let alone art that is appreciated in the world at large.

Painting has changed Seth's life. Not only has there been a shift in his autism—the attentiveness to his trips and upcoming openings,

LEFT: *Rocket Man 2*, 2008. Oil on canvas, 30 × 48 inches.

Elton John is from England. This is my painting of Elton John's Rocket Man. The Planets have many colors. The Moon is White. The Explosion has Rings and Triangles are on the circle. The Clouds have Different Hues of Reds, Violets, Teals, and Blues. The Strings have different Hues of Plums, Nectarines, Cranberries, Raspberries, Strawberries, Violets, Blues, King's Deep Blues, Dark Knight's Blues, Grayish-Purples, and Pinks. The Sky is Black. The Rocket Man feels enthusiastic and thrilled. I feel excited.

the dictations recapping his days, his increased verbalization—but his dreams are larger. He is more joyful. Every day I walk into rooms filled with color and beauty, I see my son beaming with delight, and my soul soars anew.

SETH'S FIRST MENTORS WERE WOMEN in their thirties and forties—mature artists. In January 2007 he started with three students from the Cleveland Institute of Art—young women his age, whom he loves. He calls them "same-age." They introduced him to hot pink, bright neon colors, metallic colors, and new subjects. We adored them. At first, all our openings were local. They were Seth's life events and meant the world to us.

Then in April 2007 my friend Lynda Yanks pushed me a bit. She helped me dream bigger and opened the door into yearning. How many ways was I limiting Seth by assuming this was all he could do? How would he respond to a male "same-age" mentor? Would his work become more masculine and more adult? Would studying sculpting help his painting? Could he have openings in other cities? Other countries? Were there untapped paintings in him beyond anything he was doing now? Have I considered Seth being on *Oprah*? Seth's idea of Galapagos was great. Had I considered Cayman? Seth had to snorkel and see fish. Was I letting myself dream? Did I understand? Seth could be a world icon of hope. It was my job to make this happen.

Lynda is my close friend. I trust her. I found male mentors including a sculptor. I booked Galapagos. When Seth said, "Cayman," I said "Yes." I waited to hear his dreams.

Seth definitely has dreams. Sometimes he says, "Seth will be famous. Seth will help people. Seth's art will be in hospitals. Seth's art will make people feel all better. Seth will walk on the red carpet. Seth will win awards." The dreams I had of normalcy seem distant and fragmented now. It's as if I dreamed them for another child in another lifetime. Today's dreams are robust and filled with possibility.

Dreams take hard work to make them happen. Goal number one is to have the intention. If it doesn't exist in my mind, it may never exist. Once I can imagine it, I contemplate it and break it down into baby steps. I find the turnings in the path that will take us to where we want to be. Out of the blue, Seth said to me, "Where is Oprah Winfrey? Oprah Winfrey is in Chicago. Name of building?" I didn't know. We looked up Oprah. Anyone can send a two-thousand-word e-mail, requesting to be on her show. In April 2007, we sent our two thousand words. Seth said to me, "When is Oprah?" I didn't say, "Never. It won't happen." I didn't promise, but I didn't say anything to shatter the dream. I told Seth, "We wrote to her. Maybe they'll write back soon, but maybe it won't be until the future. Maybe not until 2011. Maybe not until 2012. We will see." Maybe someday he will be on one of the shows on Oprah's new network.

I might not have taken a step toward any of these dreams if Lynda hadn't pushed me to go beyond my current comfort level. At the time she gave me a powerful nudge Seth and I were happy. Our life was the best it had ever been. I had more than I had ever dreamed of, but were my dreams too small? What did I learn from Yitzchak Schwartz, my beloved Kabbalist? To achieve our potential, we must yearn, we must yearn to be "the best, the unbelievably, most powerful best we could be." Had I done that? Had Seth? I never asked that question before. We had come so far. Maybe, just maybe, we are on the beginning of the journey and it isn't yet time to rest.

What if Seth's dreams come true? What if he meets Oprah, and some of the people on his wish list want to meet him and have his paintings? What if I work myself out of a job? What if it becomes clear

4 Griffins on an Aqua Sky,
2007. Oil on canvas
36 × 60 inches.

to the world who Seth is and there is nothing to prove or create and
now he can just paint, with artist mentors and people who love us to
do the rest? Then what about me? If my destiny is always to serve Seth,
fine. So be it. If there is another step, fine. So be it. What might I do?
What might my life be? What if I can go beyond my comfort zone? In
my career as a therapist I ran groups and workshops, was on television
and radio, and had call-in shows, happily chatting with people about
dreams, love, relationships. I have passion. What about me? Who am
I? What if the only limit to my exploring and creating was my need to
be jump-started into yearning? I yearn to create Seth's world. Could I
yearn for something more, something unknown? We are not doing this
for fame or money or power. We are doing this to become the best we
can be, to continue a legacy of the people we have loved and lost and who

Dreams II

I know are cheering us on, and to give hope to everyone and anyone who is broken and lost. We don't have a clear path. Perhaps all we need is to know we haven't hit our stride, but at least we are yearning and going in the right direction! I want peace, bliss, miracles. I want to be surprised and delighted. Count me in. I'm going on this journey.

For the first fifty years of my life, I tried to be good and do what was right. I let nothing stop me. I went to college at sixteen, finished a master's in social work at twenty-two, began working as soon as I graduated. I studied and changed and grew. I tried for five years to conceive. I had Seth. I had two miscarriages. Seth was diagnosed with autism, and I worked night and day to help him. I was physically ill. My marriage failed. I lost my mom in an automobile crash. Life was like being hit by a freight train, car after car after car. I was dealing with autism. Maybe you are not dealing with autism but you may be screaming for help, or like I was, are too stunned to cry out. We've all been beaten down. We try to cope and we get up every day and do our best. We make a plan and we stick with it. If it hasn't worked yet, maybe it will work tomorrow or next week. And then a year's gone by, a decade's gone by, and a part of life's gone by. We've been crushed, derailed, and discouraged. Maybe the plan is not going to work. Maybe our take on reality was mistaken. Sometimes we are so exhausted and defeated that we cannot stay where we are, doing the same thing and never getting the results we want, so we jump. I know I did. What I was doing wasn't working so I changed course and began to look for help down other avenues. My initial forays weren't so easy. It can be a challenge to move into the spiritual, into peace, and into wonder and awe, especially when dealing with real-life issues and struggles. It can seem like a luxury to explore these realms but I felt I had no choice. I was able to make the move through music, meditation, prayer, learning, random acts of kindness, benevolence, gratitude, journals, and dream work.

I found myself in a new place. Suddenly, my heart was full of hope, I could see beyond the day-to-day struggle and look at what could fulfill me if I only allowed it to. The reality of my life did not change, yet I feel like the luckiest person alive. I had to give up my most basic assumptions about existence, relationships, life, and love in order to gain those very things. Seth needed love, protection, guidance, fun, joy, stimulation, and to explore new horizons. I had to put my pain aside. I didn't feel like I was much stronger than Seth, but I knew I was better equipped than he was to face the world and find our way in it. I could not let him down. Focusing on his needs, which were immense, pulled me into a different reality. What could I do? Could I say, "I'm sorry, kid, you're on your own?" It didn't matter that I wasn't sure I could do it, I *had* to do it. I had to transform and become more competent, enter the unknown, and do the impossible.

I have not given up on a cure in general or a cure for Seth in particular. I continue to pray for a cure for all autistic children. I pray for all the moms receiving difficult diagnoses for any child.

We will see what life brings. Would Seth be happier as a doctor or a lawyer? Maybe. Maybe not. Would he be happier as a married man? I know he wants this. These questions are painful to contemplate. But what is, is. And what will be, will be. He is happy as he is. In fact, he is happier than almost anyone I've ever met. That counts. He has certainly had a positive effect on me. And that counts, too. It's not over yet. Maybe we will transform each other over and over.

How do I know Seth's dreams? Some of them he blurts out daily. Some of them I found out through a music therapy exercise. Twice a week he meets with Lori Smith and they work on finding ways for Seth to have meaningful conversations. We want to expand his options. We are searching for new topics that would interest Seth. Lori gives a weekly assignment, such as: "Google a topic. What did you learn?

Crocodile Rock, 2008. Oil on canvas, 18 × 24 inches.

I did 3 Abstracts of Crocodile Rock for Sir Elton John. If you know how to reach him, please tell him he can have a Rocket Man or a Crocodile Rock painting. The 3 Abstracts of Crocodile Rock have Different Shapes and Different Hues of Reds, Pumpkins, Ketchups, Buttercups, Yellows, Oranges, Browns, Chocolates, Pinks, Hot Fudges, Purples, Violets, Blues, Daffodils, Dandelions, Orange Carrots, Clementines, Tangerines, Apricots, Grays, Glow in the Dark Colors, Pansies, Coffees, Dark Oranges, Dark Greens, Dark Reds, Watermelons, Blueberries, Plums, and Purple Grapes.

What will *you* do with the new information? 1. I will talk about ____. 2. I want to paint ____. 3. Now I am interested in____." Every week Seth Googles. He lists what he has learned. (He has never once answered any of the three questions.)

I, of course, have lots of questions. I would love to know what Seth thinks, what he wants from life and how he understands his world. Seth had stopped painting for Elton John; in addition to the *Rocket Man* paintings he did three abstracts of *Crocodile Rock*. Together we

have sent a letter and prints to Elton John, hoping that he will accept one of these paintings. Seth is now creating works for Bob Dylan. I know he is painting *Blowin' in the Wind*, but I do not understand the painting. He has drawn a charcoal sketch inspired by the song, but I cannot figure out what is being depicted. It looks like trees but they are too thin. All the branches are going in the same direction. Is it flags? Too organic. Something was clearly blowing in the wind, but what? Questions like this fill my mind daily. I do not usually get answers, but this time I got a few:

> [I will talk about] *Blowin' in the Wind*. [I want to paint] tall grass wind-ing. [Now I am interested in] I will send Seth's artwork to Bob Dylan. Pictures of *Crocodile Rock* to get money. Give away to Elton John. I'll bring *Rocket Man* to Elton John.

I am confused. "To get money"? "Give away"? Is he selling them or giving them away? I ask Seth. Seth answers, "Get money from Milton Newmark to do Seth's artwork. Give away to Elton John."

Now I know more about Seth's world. My dad always gave major money to support Seth's art. Now I know that Seth understands this and appreciates this. His words are accurate. He knows it takes money to paint. He wants to give away his art to Elton John, Bob Dylan, Oprah, and Big Bird. These are his dreams.

As soon as Seth answers the second question, I realize that what is blowing in the wind is tall grass! What else could it be! It is both an abstract of tall grass and the essence of tall grass. Seth says, "The tall grass is wind-ing." What a great word. I don't know a word in the English language that means "blowing in the wind." But Seth has one. We spent twenty years pulling Seth into functional language. Maybe we needed to listen more closely to Seth and honor his way of expressing himself. Maybe his language is poetry. I was also confused by the shapes that I first thought were layered mountains. Later Seth told me they were clouds. There are hundreds of them, some less than an inch long, in blues, purples, salmons, reds, oranges, greens, and yellows. It is quite a painting. We ended up selling it to a family in Grand Cayman. Seth kept going and did a total of five *Blowin' in the Wind* paintings including *Blowin' in the Wind, Blowin' in the Wind #2,* and *Blowin' in the Wind #5.*

A NEW PERSON COMES INTO MY LIFE. One day she casually tells me that her daughter's good friend works for Oprah. Soon images of Seth's art are going to that producer. They love the art but they are booked well in advance. Do we mind waiting? We are okay with waiting. We have become accustomed to it.

My friend Lois Rose calls. She is trying to find a contact for Sid Caesar. Her son Joel, a journalist, is helping. So far she hasn't had any luck. Seth is sending e-mails to Oprah. He tells me he wants to write to Big Bird. Why not? I will back up his dream to connect with these people (and Muppet!) with every ounce of energy I have. Seth's current dreams are to meet Oprah, to bring art to these people, to be in the American Folk Art Museum on Fifth Avenue in Manhattan, and to paint the dolphins of Curaçao. A lot of what Seth wants inexplicably seems to happen. The future is starting to feel more real than the past. The "certains" started out as dreams and hopes or surprises. Now I understand it is simply a rhythm. Yesterday's dreams and surprises are today's realities. Today's dreams and surprises might be tomorrow's realities. Could it be that simple? Sometimes we get sidetracked. Seth wants to go to Malta and Greenland. There is no time. Some things

TOP RIGHT: *Blowin' in the Wind*, 2008. Oil on canvas, 18 × 24 inches.

This is painting about Bob Dylan Song. The Grass is winding. The Clouds have Different Hues of Turquoises, Teals, King's Deep Blues, Sages, Lime Greens, Ice Greens, Moonlights, Oranges, Mint Greens, Yellow-Greens, Yellow Freezes, Lilacs, and Violets. The Grass has Different hues of Lime Greens, King's Deep Blues, Kumba Greens, Green Cake Frostings, Lettuce Greens, Lake Greens, River Greens, Ocean Greens, Pond Greens, Fern Greens, and Ice Greens.

CENTER: *Blowin' in the Wind #2*, 2008. Oil on canvas, 18 × 24 inches.

The Clouds have Different Hues of Multicolored Rainbow Colors, Pinks, Grays, Butter Popcorns, Candy Apple Reds, Apple Greens, Pumpkin Pies, Strawberry Pinks, Watermelons, Strawberry Yogurts, and Cherry Reds. The Grass has Different Hues of Greens. The Grass is winding. It is a partly cloudy and partly sunny day. It is a windy day. I feel glad about this painting. I would like to give a painting to Bob Dylan.

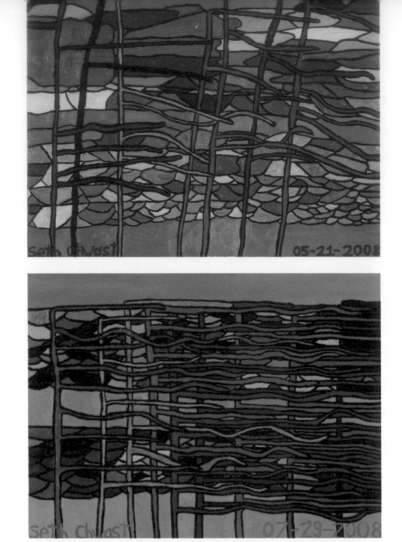

don't work. We did not return to Galapagos. We were invited to each event for the Darwin celebration but there was no way to feature Seth's art. Graham Watkins stopped working to write a book and did not go straight to a nonprofit in Africa. So, we are not on our way to Africa. Not every seed comes to fruition. The possibilities excite and encourage us, but they are often replaced by something equally, or even more, wonderful. However, some dreams are becoming our new realities.

When I do things for Seth, it is not simply so that he will have a good time. Of course, I am thrilled when things go well and he is happy. But my motivation is to keep him stimulated, joyful, and interested in the world. Why do I listen to Seth's dreams? Because the paintings pour out? Because Lynda said he and I have a job to do? Because the alternative was dry mopping? Because I am following in Darwin's footsteps, keeping my eyes, mind, and heart open? To see where life will take us? Yes. All of the above.

My goal is to protect Seth beyond my grave. I want to take my energy, gifts, passion, and knowledge and pour them into supporting and creating his world. Seth leads, I follow. When my will is to do his will, magic happens. On good days, we're in a rhythm and Seth creates his art and he is happy. On bad days, people tell me no one can successfully contact superstar celebrities or museums. People look at me with pity and concern. Our dreams are sometimes met with scorn. All I can do is put one foot in front of the other and keep going. Logic and reality don't always work for us.

I do not know where we will be in a year. I believe it will be wonderful. I believe it will be different from what I know and expect. I think it will be better. I feel like I started planting seeds in the summer of 2003, filled with blind hope. And now it is starting to feel like tomatoes and zucchini in mid-summer. Bursting with life and possibility.

OPPOSITE BOTTOM: *Blowin' in the Wind #5*, 2008. Oil on canvas, 18 × 24 inches.

I like painting "Blowin' in the Wind" for Bob Dylan. The Grass has Different Hues of Greens. The Clouds have Different Hues of Pinks, Reds, Roses, Beets, Grapes, Oranges, Violets, Tangerines, and Cantaloupes. I feel glad about this painting.

CHAPTER 9
Expecting the Unexpected

Before Seth was twelve, when we were still hoping for the therapies to work and make him normal, we were in Atlanta with our dear friends Lis and Nick at a public pool, and Lis said to me, "I want you to meet this kid. He's eighteen and autistic." Every cell in my body screamed, "No!" I could not believe that any young adult could still be autistic. These memories take my breath away. How could I have been so blind, so sheltered, and so out of touch? My heart aches for the woman and mother that I was back then. I read the autism miracle books about the children who had been transformed into normalcy, but only after their parents worked hard enough, got the right team, went to Switzerland for a month, to Japan for two years, and so on. The message seemed to be: *Do this and you, too, can be, or will be, the mom of a kid who is no longer autistic.* Seth was born in 1983 and he was the only autistic person in his graduating class. We did not have role models. We became the role model. If I could go back and speak to my former self I'd tell her to read those books and pull any advice or hope she could from them, but also to slow down and breathe, to plan, to search, and to hope for both a more realistic and a greater dream. Blind and desperate, loyal and determined, blessed and walking between the raindrops, I am trying to give Seth a great life. I hope our story, my pain and Seth's bliss, can make reality shift a bit for those struggling to find their balance.

After Seth's diagnosis, I was confused. I unknowingly defined a good life—success and happiness—by whether or not we could fight hard enough, try hard enough, be devoted enough to cure, reverse, or break through the autism. In reality, Seth was autistic. I was not. Either of us could have had a horrible life or a great life. How could I not have

Roller Coaster, detail from *Manhattan Floating*, 2010. Acrylic on canvas, 32 × 24 inches.

169

known this? Are all my normal friends happy? Are all their twenty-
and thirty-year-old children happy? Would I have believed there was
something other than the goal of normalcy if, when Seth was four, I
had met the woman I have now become and met Seth as he is now? We
really, really, really want our kids to be normal. May it happen for all of
us in the myriad of ways that it can.

In 2006, an op-ed piece in the *New York Times* cited that in the span
of one month three parents had killed their autistic children, including
a woman who had held her child's hand as they jumped off a bridge in a
homicide-suicide. One parent was a physician. All had read the miracle
cure books. All were turning their worlds upside down, devoting their
lives to fighting autism and bringing in teams of people to stimulate their
child. And, after giving up reality as they knew it, following directions
day and night, overextending themselves financially and emotionally,
their children were still autistic. They could not see beyond the autism.
They could not see beyond the "nevers" and the "nos" that rained down
on them and their precious children. My heart is heavy for those families
who saw no other way. There is no doubt that the journey with an autistic
child is arduous, exhausting, and depleting. I knew there seemed to be
miracle cures but now I wish there had been something that would have
encouraged me to try, promised nothing, and held my hand if in the end,
I found myself in a world without a miracle cure. I needed to know that
would be okay, too. I needed to know that we could have a different life,
and that it could be a great life.

WE ARE NOT A COMMERCIAL SUCCESS. We are not making money
or coming close to breaking even. We're not a business. Art is Seth's
therapy. It is how he improves and moves forward every day of his life.

It is what motivates him to communicate. It helps him develop a work ethic. It empowers him and helps him make choices on every level. It makes him happy. Hundreds of times a day he can pick a specific color, a specific brush. He can work on a Pegasus or sculpt a Neptune riding a hippocampus or paint a dolphin. He can decide if he's stopping at 5:00 p.m., as he usually does, or if he wants to paint with another mentor for two hours after dinner. He has a world and can control it. We do his e-mail together for about an hour a day. He is connected to people. He is part of the community of the world.

For years, we searched for a reason to get up every day. We were on a quest to discover a way to meet friends, interact with colleagues,

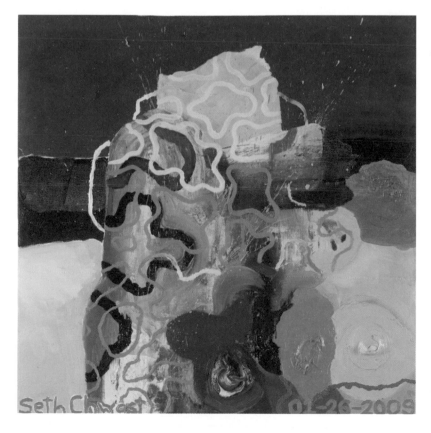

Abstract in Oil 01-26-2009, 2009. Oil on canvas, 20 × 20 inches.

Wow! The Abstract Shapes have Different Hues of Ice Greens, Teals, Turquoises, Luminous Operas, Reds, Ketchups, Burgundies, Ruby Reds, Burgundy Reds, Yellow-Greens, Greens, Fleshes, Green Licorices, Purples, Purple Grapes, Ultramarine Blues, Luminous Oranges, and Whites. I signed in White and then I signed in Red-Orange over the White. I made Imaginary Shapes with Different Hues of Yellow Ochres, Yellows, Whites, and Reds.

be seen, appreciated, feel useful, and become who we were meant to be and feel grateful for it. For Seth it was art. It could have been anything. It could have been chocolate chip cookies. If it had been, we would have immersed ourselves in a world of searching for the perfect ingredients, hosting cookie-tasting parties, making gifts, finding customers, exploring shipping, and developing a website. I wish someone had told me about this kind of happy ending.

So how is the journey coming along, of birthing ourselves into the best we can be? What is the autism like today? How does it affect our lives? Seth finished *The Two Iguana* (see page 108) on July 5, 2009. It is oil on canvas, 30 by 40 inches, and it took him 250 hours. That is not a guess or an estimate. We record the time it takes for him to complete his paintings. That week I watched him work on his 104-panel painting of *Manhattan Floating*. He was on his third panel of buildings. He had mixed the light green for a window and was doing what the Cleveland Institute of Art students call "grabbing paint." There was a glob of paint on the palette and Seth was collecting tiny specks of it from the periphery. He was grinning and gleeful and grabbing paint molecule by molecule. I was watching in disbelief.

Seth is not a robot. He was not put on this earth to knock out paintings. He enjoys what he does. At first, when he moves to the canvas, he is not what art students call "making marks." Although it looks like he is painting, I know he is really cleaning his brush on the canvas. He hates it when paint gets on the metal part of the brush, so he is using the canvas to clean his brush. This takes about a minute. When the brush is clean enough to make him happy, then he finally starts to paint. I would guess that half of his time painting is spent gathering specks of paint and cleaning his brush on the canvas. When he is doing this, I think he is being autistic—doing what is called stimming, getting lost in obsessive repetitive actions. I asked Harris, his main Cleveland mentor, what he does when Seth is playing with paint rather than painting. He said he lets Seth play for a while and then interrupts him. I simply watch. I have no answer. I know there are 104 panels of *Manhattan Floating* to finish and it will take over a year. But I also know that Seth is in bliss and squeals in delight as he plays with the paint. Seth has plenty of time to play with paint, and there is always time for lots of giggling and bliss.

Seth had already finished *The Hippocampus Coming into the East River*, four panels in the bottom left corner of the New York painting. It took forty-six hours. That section was finished, photographed, and archived. Not so fast. Seth decided he wanted bubbles floating up

Hippocampus under the Water, detail from *Manhattan Floating*, 2010. Acrylic on canvas, 32 × 48 inches.

through the water. So the four finished *Manhattan Floating* panels that have already been photographed and archived, now got bubbles and went back to be re-archived. Next he worked on *The Red Sea Turtle*, another four-panel section. After making bubbles in this painting, he added silver highlights, a crescent on top of each bubble. They are splendid. So he went back a second time to the finished *Hippocampus* to highlight the bubbles he had put there, which took another sixteen hours. The *Hippocampus* went back again to be photographed and archived. And it will be finished, again. But it was worth it because the bubbles are amazing. Later, Seth outlined the *Hippocampus* in black and it was archived for a fourth time. There is no way to stop Seth from going back to these paintings if he feels they need more work.

In the summer of 2009, Seth began an incredible series of dolphin paintings, spurred on by the visit from Karen Stary of the Dolphin Heart

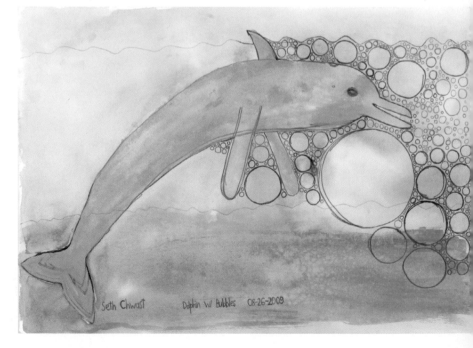

RIGHT: *Dolphin with Bubbles*, 2009. Graphite with acrylic wash on Rives paper, 10.75 × 15 inches.

OPPOSITE: *The Orange Macaroni and Cheese Dolphin*, 2009. Acrylic on oven-baked clay, 6.5 × 10 × 8.5.

Foundation, who was trying to arrange for a trip to the Curaçao
Dolphin Therapy and Research Center. All Seth needed
to hear was the word dolphin. Soon he was painting a
dolphin for *Manhattan Floating*. Whether we would go to
Curaçao or not, at least we would have one lovely dolphin
swimming in the East River! But on November 2, 2009, it
was settled. We would go to Curaçao on December 5 for nine
days. Ann and Ken and the kids were coming.

Curaçao was a dream come true. Seth was assigned to Mateo, a large
male dolphin, and Marco, the head trainer. For two hours a day, they
slipped into a different reality. Seth hummed, squealed, and laughed.
Mateo whistled, clicked, and squeaked. In our world, Seth has trouble
with the rhythm of conversation. He can be silent or he can pour out
roller coaster or construction information. Many moms of autistic kids
spend hours upon hours trying to "complete circles." I talk, you respond,
I respond. At age twenty-seven, Seth had finally met his circle buddy, and
it was a dolphin. He and Mateo took turns, never interrupted each other,
and made circles nonstop. They were communicating about and planning
when to swim, when to stop, and what to do next. They did it without
using a single word. Marco reported that after ten minutes he pulled back;
Seth and Mateo were fine without him. Marco didn't know if it was Mateo
or Seth leading, just that they were connecting and communicating in
their own way. Seth, who is afraid of butterflies and would rather paint
animals than touch them, looked like he was born to swim with dolphins.
He held on to Mateo as they swam around the lagoon. Seth previously
had no interest in sign language, but now when he was shown the sign to
make Mateo speak, he used it over and over until he collapsed into a belly
laugh that we had never heard before. Seth liked one of the other three
therapy dolphins as well, a female named Li-Na. The dolphins pulled
Seth through the lagoon as he shrieked with laughter.

While we were in Curaçao, we met Kiki from Dolphin Aid in Germany. The organization sponsored our visit and has helped children beyond count. Kiki's son's life was changed by dolphin therapy. This place is her dream, her passion. When she watched Seth and Mateo in the water, she could see immediately that they were communicating. We also met with Krissy, the founder of the Curaçao Autism Society, a bouncy, warm, friendly woman who adored Seth's art and invited us back for Thanksgiving 2011. Seth will be the featured artist for an autism awareness week. The next day Michèle Russell-Capriles took us to her gallery, Landhuis-Bloemhof, on the land her family has owned since the 1500s when, as Jews, they fled from Spain. She is as warm and loving as she is efficient and knowledgeable. Seth will open in her gallery in November 2011. These people are starting to feel like family.

When we got home, Seth seemed more adult, more certain, more self-determining. He wanted more field trips and told us each day what he wants to do. We entered a more peaceful time. Seth wanted more leisurely mornings, longer lunches, and a more spontaneous life. I think in Mateo, Seth finally met a bright, interesting being who understood him within minutes. Bypassing what we call language, they had communication that was functional and joyful. I think it transformed Seth. Soon we had a *Trio of Dolphins* in the East River and *The Orange Fantasy Dolphin in the Night Sky*.

Was Curaçao and dolphin therapy a vacation for me? Ann was concerned that I never relax. She told me that my life never changes. I can be at home, in New York, or in Curaçao and I am working on Seth's world—e-mails, openings, archiving, scheduling. It never stops. We should take a vacation like we did in March 2007 when we went to Costa Rica. At that time, I had never dreamed of art openings outside of America and life was slower. In the chill of December 2009, a vacation sounded like a good idea, and we began to review our options. Seth

The Orange Fantasy Dolphin in the Night Sky, 2010. Acrylic on canvas, 24 × 18 inches.

The Dolphin has Different Hues of Yellows, Daffodils, Bananas, Pineapples, Lemons, Yellow Squashes, Mangoes, Mango Sherbets, Grapefruits, Yellow Bell Peppers, Potatoes, French Fries, Tater Tots, Hash Browns, Latkes, Potato Chips, Yellow Watermelons, Yellow Roses, Sunflowers, Dandelions, Corns, Corn Chips, Corn Cakes, Corn Puddings, Taco Shells, Tortilla Chips, Nachos, Butters, Butter-Flavored Popcorns, Corn Pancakes, Corn Muffins, Swiss Cheeses, Banana Cream Pies, Banana Puddings,

Yellow Cake Frostings, Lemonades, Yellow Sun, Yellow Venus, Honey, Cheesecakes, Yellow Fireworks, Oranges, Orange Popsicles, Orange Juices, Orangeades, Orange Drinks, Orange Sodas, Tangerines, Cantaloupes, Macaroni and Cheeses, American Cheeses, Cheddar Cheeses, Carrots, Yams, Sweet Potatoes, Carrot Soups, Apricots, Marmalades, Goldfishes, Goldfish Cheese Crackers, Orange Bell Peppers, Orange Cake Frostings, Orange Sherbets, Marigolds, Orange Poppies, Orange Fireworks ,and Whites. The Dolphin feels excited and gleeful.

poured over websites. I read travel books. Seth picked Machu Picchu, and we scheduled Peru for June 24, 2010.

Kip flew to Cleveland for the first time in January 2010. In one week, he transformed Seth's main workspace into a professional studio. Life went on. Donna relocated. Kip became Seth's primary mentor. He organizes and inspires us. He is pure magic in our lives.

People ask me, "What do the mentors do?" The first thing they do is keep Seth safe. He needs to be monitored every minute. He gets lost in time. He cannot be in a house alone. He cannot eat alone. Because he doesn't understand the technical aspects of putting paint tube caps back on, covering a palette with plastic wrap so the paint does not dry out, or cleaning brushes, somebody has to do that for him. Somebody must always be in the room for Seth to paint. I don't know if he wants the company or if he lacks confidence. I do know he won't paint without a mentor. All of the artists/mentors who work with Seth think of him as an artist but also have to take into consideration that he is autistic and explore ways to help him move forward with his art.

The autism might double the time it takes for each painting to be completed. On the other hand, it may be why Seth can focus so intensely. When Seth is taking ninety seconds to grab paint, it's the autism. But it may also be the autism when he does *The Dutch Master*, a black-and-white 40-by-60-inch drawing on which he spent hours making thousands of tiny hatch marks to create a multitude of patterns. The piece came about when Kip printed out an image of a painting by a minor Dutch artist, most likely a contemporary of Rembrandt's, and asked Seth to make a drawing of it. The result seems half Dutch master and half the whimsical faces from *The Yellow Submarine*. Seth often paints daily. The autism, to be honest, makes the amount of time he devotes to his art possible. His mentors spend time on relationships and the responsibilities of families, friends, work, and life in general. For them, reality cuts into the time they can spend on their art. What Seth cannot do, which is most of these things, frees him for what he can do. Which is to paint.

Seth has talent. He is a colorist and a gifted artist. He is as certain in his art as he is lost in the social world. We are a team. He has the artistic talent and I made the choice to take my talents and gifts and focus them on creating a space where Seth can blossom. I lived in New York, went to school in Berkeley, traveled, and had an exciting life. Now most days I eat dinner at six in the evening, am asleep by ten, and get up at six in the morning. For me, a really good day is two to eight hours of organizing and developing the world of Seth's art along with time to contemplate loving the green of the grass and the blue of the sky and filling with gratitude. It is a quiet life. Around me I have Seth's painting mentors—women with orange or cranberry red hair or shaved heads, zany socks, striped tights, tattoos, and multiple piercings; men with long hair or shaved heads, tattoos, funky clothing, and fixie bikes. It's not what I am used to, but I love it. I love them. I bless them and I'm grateful every day they show up. I do all I can to support, sustain, and encourage them.

Things have been a little more exciting of late. I still do the never-ending planning and details, the quiet behind-the-scenes work, but I no longer feel so reclusive. A really good day now includes some outrageous travel planning.

Machu Picchu was all we hoped for and more. When I saw the Andes I felt a profound joy beyond words. I knew that all of our efforts were worth it. Every day we took a long drive to a ruin, spent time exploring, and took a long drive home. For me, the drives were magical. I wanted only to see those mountains. I felt such a sense of peace. I felt like I had come home. Seth was euphoric.

It wasn't easy. Someone still had to watch Seth every moment. It took six months of planning. I worked on my health in preparation for such a strenuous trip, going to see several doctors and walking more and

The Dutch Master, 2008.
Pencil on paper,
40 × 60 inches.

I made [a version] of a
Dutch Master oil paint-
ing. I did a different
background. The People
have Clothes have differ-
ent patterns. The Ground
has many lines. The
Background has grass
with different lines. The
Dutch Master used paint
and many colors. I used
pencil and many patterns.
The People feel excited.
It is very hard to do this
drawing. I like Black-and-
White Drawing.

10-07-2008

more each day. Once in Peru, I struggled. The altitude is a challenge and the climbs are not easy. Each night I thought, *I did it.* In the end, I made it through every day. Once, I was very ill for two hours. We did a difficult climb, and I had abdominal pain and thought I'd pass out. Ann took me back down. Seth went ahead with the guide, Ken, and the kids. Soon I was fine. We do not travel like most people do. We had our own van, our own driver, and our own guide, and went at our own pace. Our guide said I could never have kept up with a normal tour. Taking our time, we did every single ruin. We got to Machu Picchu. I came home with increased confidence about taking myself and Seth into the world.

As soon as we got home from Peru, Seth said, "Rio and Buenos Aires." Hmm, I was contemplating Morocco in March, which I thought was pretty wild. Now Seth wanted Rio. Would it be too much? Would it be irresponsible? For two weeks I was torn. Would the money or my health run out first? But then I started to think about my mom. Some of my best memories include our trips together. It is still shocking to me that she was fine one day and gone the next. Seth wants to go to Rio, Morocco, Italy, and Easter Island. It would be prudent to go to one place a year, but what if my health doesn't allow for four great years? Right now I feel wonderful. Health might be the more precious commodity.

For thirty years, I lacked energy and had gastrointestinal issues. When I reported the fatigue to doctors, it was suggested I exercise more and get more sleep. I think some of my doctors thought the cause of my symptoms was emotional. I found a new level of help when I flew to Duluth, Minnesota, to see Virginia Shapiro, the functional medicine practitioner who had helped us with Seth. I wanted her to see Seth and my dad, and, as a lark, to see me. After our examination, she was concerned: "You are very ill. You go out for a really nice early supper. Then you'll fast tonight, I'll open my office in the morning, and we'll do blood work." I replied, "I am not ill." Every doctor since 1971 had said I was not ill. We did the blood work. I was ill.

We flew home. My primary doctor ordered a sonogram and an MRI. He saw the results and told my then-husband that I'd be dead in three weeks. No one told me. When I didn't die, they knew that the tumor—7 by 7 inches and 5 inches deep—in the middle of my liver and pressing on my internal organs was benign.

But there was no treatment.

In 2003 I returned to Virginia Shapiro for help with diet and supplements. She asked question after question about my bowels, asked if I'd been to Africa, got on the Internet, called colleagues, and wondered if I might have parasites. She suggested a physician who could treat me for liver flukes. The tumor might actually be the cells that the flukes build and hatch out of. There would be no way to know for certain without a needle biopsy. The tumor was vascular. The biopsy could kill me. Did I want to just treat for parasites? Absolutely. I saw the doctor and took the pills. Since 2003, I have slowly and steadily been improving. I was so ill and so debilitated, recovering is like climbing Everest. I am climbing every day.

If I had liver flukes, I had been incrementally poisoned a little more each day for thirty years, ever since I drank the water during a trip to Africa in 1971. I lived the life I could, the life of the mind, the spirit, and the soul. I was a kind and loving mom, daughter, friend, and therapist. I did it all without much strength. Now I am feeling better every day. I want the thirty years back that I felt ill, but that isn't going to happen. If my luck holds out, the next few years will be splendid. If it doesn't, at least I tried my best. I am filled with passion and have an insatiable need for travel and fun. I am dreaming of places like Easter Island. Physical problems may hold me back but I am willing to take the chance and make plans.

I wish I could take Seth all over the world. I am not great with jet lag, so it is much easier to travel within as few time zones as possible. Heat or humidity are difficult for me, so Rio has to be in September or October; Easter Island has to be in December or March. I can't do four-wheel drive as it is too bumpy, so I need paved roads. I can't take malaria pills, so there goes Belize. If it is Rio, it is impossibly soon. Ann is torn about leaving her family. The kids will be in school and can't come. Ken has no more vacation time. I have five books on Brazil, four on Argentina, some on Morocco, and a few on Italy. Morocco is a four-hour time difference, which is probably manageable, and there is no need for malaria medication, and there are paved roads. On August 12, Ann decided to go with us to Rio de Janeiro and Buenos Aires, and we booked a trip for October 1, 2010. I am back to walking morning and night to keep myself in shape. I do not recognize the person I've become. Or maybe this is who I always was, and I just did not know it.

It may seem like we are simply taking a vacation to Rio but this trip is much more than that. For me, it is a journey into a world where we may be limited, but not stopped, by autism and my illness. The first time we traveled with Seth it seemed impossible. Ann and I couldn't wrap our brains around getting him or me out of the country. Now it is our reality. I want to see the world. I want to bring Seth and his art into the world. I attempted to contact the three autism organizations in Rio; their e-mails no longer function. Do they still exist? Can they speak English? I sent letters by regular mail. We were cherished when Seth exhibited in Galapagos and Cayman. We were embraced and scheduled for an opening in Curaçao. I want to reach out and bring Seth, his art, and our message of hope wherever we go. It might happen in Rio. It might not. We will send the letters out into the world and see what comes back to us.

Expecting the Unexpected

As much as Seth's autism held us back until our first trip in 2007, now it opens doors. We are moving from being tourists to being travelers, and maybe ambassadors for autism. We still get e-mails from two of our Costa Rican guides. One has an autistic son, and he brought us to his house to meet him. The other was a young man who simply liked us and was happy when Seth asked for his e-mail. Seth continues to get warm letters from Silvia, who sold roller coaster tickets in Ecuador. An artist in Curaçao introduced us to his autistic son and gave Seth a beautiful little sculpture of a bicycle. His wife wrote a long letter about how inspired they are by Seth's art. He gives them hope. Whether we have formal openings and autism events or simply make friends one at a time, it is starting to feel like the world is our home.

Seth finished *Manhattan Floating*. It took fifteen months. Now he is creating painted wooden cutouts to hang as mobiles in front of the painting and/or to be placed in dioramas in front if it. Out pour the icons of Manhattan that never got into the mural: the alligators in the sewer system, the ice cream trucks, the hot dog vendors, the vintage cars, and the taxi cabs. Then along come cutouts echoing images in his painting: *The Maroon Fantasy Dragon with Pink Wings, The Lime Green Car-Plane, The Green Submarine,* and *Red Barge with Buildings.* This is a project without end. It can (and probably will) continue to evolve until the painting leaves us to go to New York City.

As another academic year ends, the CIA mentors come and go. They work with Seth in different media. Noah and Seth work with oven-bake clay. Seth makes a sculpture—a dragon, say—from aluminum foil, covers it with clay, works on details (textures such as skin and claws), and then they bake it in the oven. Once it cools, Seth gessoes and paints it. We meet a wonderful woman, Leni, who graduated from the Cleveland Institute of Art but is staying in Cleveland. She is a sculptor. She brings real clay, has Seth sculpt, and then covers the sculpture with wet cloth to seal it until she returns. With her, Seth made the first of a series of *chupacabra*, the mythical Mexican goatsucker. She took it to a kiln and then had Seth paint directly on it so he could see the colors and not yet have to deal with the ambiguity of glazes. He then experimented with mixed media and decorated his sculpture with paper and glitter. Soon we had a ten-inch creature standing on two legs, one hip jaunting out to the side, with huge ears and a beautiful tail. It took one day for the body, one day for the tail (redone three times), four hours for the mouth, one day for the ears and wings, and one day for the "fur," indicated by impossibly tiny marks. Seth was just getting started. Two more *chupacabra* soon followed.

In August 2010 we applied for a grant. Last year we applied for the same grant and one judge said Seth's work was pure and heartfelt but untrained. I went over the application with Kip, who felt I should write about Seth's lack of training before he is judged. Kip asked if I have heard of Jean-Michel Basquiat? I had not. He sent me three images of canvases of cars and planes that look quite like Seth's. These paintings are selling for over one million dollars. Do I know the works of David Hockney? Yes. Do I understand that Seth and David Hockney have similar landscapes? No. Could I please go and look at the sky on *Coney Island Cyclone*? (See page 69.) Do I understand that Seth paints like Basquiat or Hockney although he has never seen their work? This is better than emulating them. Like them, Seth uses his painting as a vocabulary to portray his sensibilities.

Seth painted the same happy horse with impossibly short, thin legs in twenty-one different paintings. Colors change, details change, they are clearly a family. Several art students tell me this is a problem, Seth isn't growing. What do I know? I love *Apricot Cheesy Fantasy Horse*

with *Blue Sky and Peach Ground* and *Periwinkle Blue Fantasy Horse on Nectarine Land with a Bright Yellow Gold Sky.* Seth is happy. Kip has a different take on it. He says, "Seth likes to immerse himself in studies of specific subject matter that continue to evolve. Artists do that. Think of Monet and the water lilies." Seth did not get the grant. Working on the essay for the grant, I have already gained peace of mind. Kip has helped me understand Seth's art. It is flat, childlike, and repetitive. And he *is* comparable to Jean-Michel Basquiat and David Hockney. There will be no more pushing Seth to be a realist. Seth will follow his passion.

An Unexpected Life

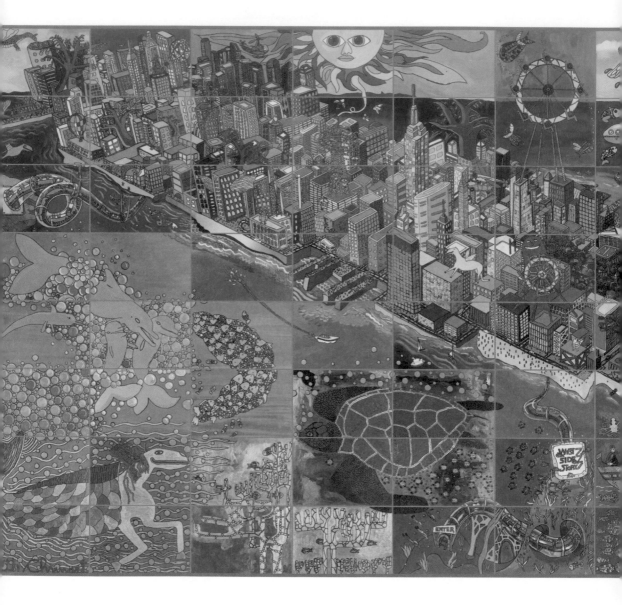

188

There is no end to the complexity of Seth's life or planning for his future. We have my last will and testament, we have plans, and someday Ann will take Seth. Every time we travel, we review our plans. One day I wonder what would happen if Seth lost me *and* Ann. If I were gone, Ann and her family would move into our home. There is no way to replace a mother when the love flows and pours both ways, but with Ann it would be a wonderfully smooth transition. Seth adores her. She already manages his trust and our home. She is here daily. Without Ann, could Ken manage his family, Seth, and Seth's career? Ann thinks not. We discussed the possibilities and then I called Kip.

I hope to live to 120. I hope Ann lives to 120. But I asked Kip if he would take Seth, if anything went wrong. He didn't hesitate. He asked no questions. He said yes. Kip spoke to his wife and she said of course they would take Seth, she loves him. It's a done deal. Kip lives in an old warehouse in Brooklyn with twenty-nine apartments. He owns three of them. If anything happened, he would put Seth and a caretaker in one of his apartments. He and Seth would eat breakfast together, decide what to paint, paint all day, have dinner together, and then Seth would go to his own apartment and Kip to his family. Kip has had commissions or openings in England, France, Morocco, and Uruguay. He has traveled for his art to Costa Rica, Belize, Argentina, Spain, and Japan and then created paintings inspired by those countries for openings in New York, Philadelphia, and California. He said he would take Seth with him to paint for weeks at a time in other countries. He would also take Seth to all the places I was not strong enough to get to. They could go to China, Thailand, and India.

Now that we had these plans, why wait? I told Kip I would send Seth any place Kip goes, when Kip has a commission. I asked Kip to start to travel with us. He and his wife have a baby and his mother-in-law comes up from Argentina to help. She will be coming every few

OPPOSITE TOP: *Apricot Cheesy Fantasy Horse with Blue Sky and Peach Ground*, 2008. Acrylic on wood, 25 × 48 inches.

The Sky is Blue. The Ground is Peach. The Mane and Tail are wavy. The Apricot Horse has texture. I feel Proud! The Horse is excited. The Lips are Orange and Peach! I feel happy!

OPPOSITE BOTTOM: *Periwinkle Blue Fantasy Horse on Nectarine Land with a Bright Yellow Gold Sky*, 2008. Acrylic on wood, 25 × 48 inches.

The Sun is yellow. The Sky is texture. I Feel happy. Horse feels Glad.

months. We decide that once a year, while she is in Brooklyn with Kip's wife and daughter, he and Seth and I will take one trip a year with Ann and her family, one trip just with Seth and Ann, and one trip with Kip. That way, if Kip is ever in the position of being responsible for Seth, they will both be more prepared to be with each other. I ask him again if he is sure he can take Seth, and he answers "He will have a great life. Do not worry." I believe in him.

Life changes. Ann's kids grew up and became three beautiful, talented, actualized individuals, all going in many directions at once. It slowly became clear that Ann could barely keep up with her own three, let alone take on Seth and his career. At the same time, Kip was becoming increasingly involved with Seth. We were talking nightly. His ideas for Seth were never ending. Seth and Kip were bonding. Seth was asking for Kip daily. One day, everything crystallized, and we all knew Seth should go to Kip. I asked Seth if he wanted to be with Kip someday and Seth said "future is Kip." Kip is five years younger than Ann, and twelve years older than Seth. Time to call our lawyer and once again protect Seth every way I can.

The first fifty years of my life I tried doing what I wanted and had fair results. Now I do what Seth wants and try to do whatever I came to earth to do and I have spectacular results. We have an unexpected life. Yes, we had hard times. Years later our quest makes for some incredible stories. *Remember the time Seth tried special needs skiing and was almost decapitated by the rope tow?* There are stories beyond count. When Seth was seven and he was learning about maps, we took him to the United Nations to buy flash cards of the flags of different countries. The cast of characters on that trip included me, Seth, Yreka the service dog, and my mom. The guard said we couldn't bring a dog into a public building. I explained disability law and that Yreka was a service dog for my son. He responded that disability laws applied only in America. Because the United Nations was not technically on U.S. soil, the dog had to stay outside. So my mom and Seth went to the shop while I remained behind with the dog. The guard kept an eye on Yreka and me the whole time. Finally, when Seth and my mom came out, the guard saw them and walked over to us. Sheepishly, he told us he had lied. Whether or not to let the dog in was too complicated for him and he didn't know how to handle it. He especially didn't want to get in trouble with his boss, so he lied. I thanked him for telling me the truth. It's easy to think that

Silver Pinto Pegasus Flying over Golden Sand and Ocean Waves with Brain Coral, 2009. Acrylic on canvas, 18 × 24 inches.

The Pegasus has Different Hues of Very, Very Light Brown. The Pegasus has Silver Spots. The Pegasus is flying in The Sky. The Pegasus's Wings has Many Feathers. The Powerful Wind is blowing the Pegasus's Mane and Tail. The Sand has many of textures. The Sand is made out of Golden Shells. The Ocean Water has many of textures on the waves. The Ocean Water has Different Hues of Blue-Greens. I used Different Brushstrokes about the Waves. The Brain Corals have many of textures. The Brain Corals have different designs of imaginary shapes. The Brain Corals have Different Tones of Silver and White. My painting's horizontal line is curvy. The Pegasus feels calm and excited! Silver Pinto I feel talented about this painting!

everyone else has all the answers and knows just what to do and how to do it. But sometimes what to do is muddy and ambiguous and you don't know and no one else knows and, right or wrong, you have to pick a path.

We simply choose to keep going. The first time Seth was on the *Today* show, a mom called me from Oregon. Her son was so compromised, could she dare hope? "Seth started painting at twenty." "Yes, but you don't understand, my son is eight and still has poop accidents." I let her know, "Oh, Seth did that, too." On the other end of the phone she began weeping with exhaustion, relief, and hope. A little bit of that hope may carry her and her son onto a path of discovery that is right for them. One of my friends took her autistic son to Costa Rica for the first of a series of stem cell treatments. She doesn't know how much it will work, but for the first time, at age twelve, he is dry through the night. What pregnant woman, anticipating the achievements of her future child, imagines joy at having a son who for the first time at age twelve doesn't wet himself throughout the night? Our victories are in worlds we did not even know existed. No matter how mundane or easy for someone else, they are victories.

Seth is not his autism. But the autism is here with us every hour of every day. It brings challenges. It brings gifts. The challenges almost destroyed me and made me who I am today. The gifts have taken me on unexpected journeys both spiritual and physical and also made me who I am today. I have learned to live with paradox. The challenges of my own illness have also almost destroyed me and I feel vulnerable much of the time. I wish I was young and strong and could run up mountains. Instead I have walked slowly and crawled when I needed to. I want you to know that if I can do it, you can do it, too. I am sure you have much more energy and strength than I do. While I often feel good, I can't do all I want to do.

Physically, when things are at their worst, I feel like a being without a body. I have tried to find health and healing with traditional medicine and alternative therapies. I have danced with acupuncture, quigong, tai chi, Rolfing, and massotherapy. Although I live in Cleveland, I've had doctors in Portland, Maine, and have followed Virginia Shapiro from Duluth, Minnesota, to Corvallis, Oregon. Between Virginia Shapiro and Tom Taxman, I am in good hands. Things are turning around. I cannot yet leap tall buildings but I am, since 2003, improving. I don't see a limit on how far I can go. By the summer of 2010, Seth and I are continuing to move into health. I have more energy. Virginia has several protocols to help me with jet lag and thinks I can take Seth to Italy. Seth, too, has seen a major improvement. I have gratitude and hope. Mostly I focus on the present, working for today to be a wonderful day and doing everything I can to make it great.

If Seth's art ends up in museums, and sale of his work ultimately supports us, I would not be surprised. If he has a few loyal collectors, mostly among my friends, and he brings hope to strangers, but never once in his life comes close to financially breaking even, I would feel that he and I lived a great life. I think Seth is an icon of hope. I do everything I can to promote my son. So far he is relatively unknown, but I believe that he has an important message. I also believe that his message will make its way out into the world and can bring healing, hope, and joy. I think all art has the ability to connect with something deep inside each of us. With Seth's art there is something more. It's not that he is simply creating Outsider Art. His art comes from a place inside of him that cannot be reached by ordinary means of conversation. Art has given him a voice, and it speaks clearly to anyone who views one of his canvases. The message may be different for each viewer but Seth's art moves people in ways that the most eloquent speaker cannot.

From the beginning, Seth's art brought him into the world and helped him make connections. His openings are his life events. He may not have a college graduation, a wedding, a baby shower, or a

housewarming party. But he has already opened at Penn State College of Medicine, University Hospitals of Case Western Reserve University, the Cleveland Clinic, the United Nations, the Royal Palm in Galapagos, the National Gallery of the Cayman Islands, the Cleveland Museum of Natural History, and the Time Equities, Inc. building in New York City. He is scheduled for openings at the Hitchcock-Dartmouth Medical Center, Curaçao, and Kiev. After the International Arts Residency at Art Omi, he was reviewed as "one of three outstanding American artists." He did the cover art for three books: *Pediatric Gastrointestinal Disorders*; *The Ethics of Autism*, which used parts of *Six Self Studies*; and *Mental Health Promotion, Prevention, and Intervention in Children and Youth: A Guiding Framework for Occupational Therapy*. He has been featured in two documentaries. He has been on the *Today* show twice. Seth has life events and each event fills him with excitement. Sometimes I ask Seth, "How do you feel?" Seth replies, "I feel gleeful. I feel happy. I feel excited." Every milestone makes him visible to families looking for hope and people inside and outside the autistic community who resonate with color and joy. We live an unexpected life.

OPPOSITE: *Abstract in Oil 03-02-2009*, 2009. Oil on canvas, 20 × 20 inches.

The Crosshatch paint has Different Hues of Zucchinis, Pickles, Cucumbers and Green Lettuce Salads. The Crosshatch has Red over Purple. The Marks have Different Hues of Yellow School Buses. The Marks have Hot Pinks. The Splatters have Teals. I used thick painting for Dark Green. I like this painting.

LEFT: *The Village: Teal Cadillac Car*, 2009. Acrylic on wood cutout, 3.5 × 11 inches.

The Vintage Cadillac with People is driving in New York City.

Acknowledgments

I'd like to acknowledge some of the people who support and champion us. Let's do this chronologically.

Francis Greenburger and my dad had a bond beyond time and space. For love of my father, Francis is kind enough to include me and my son in the group of people he cares about and protects. Seth e-mails him every few weeks and Francis always writes back. Seth thinks of Francis as his friend. Francis decided there should be a book about Seth and connected me with his literary agency, Sanford J. Greenburger Associates, Inc. Francis was the first person to read an early version of this book and encouraged me to keep going. Over and over he has come through for us in ways beyond my wildest dreams.

Anne Hawkins is my oldest friend. We met when I was sixteen, as college freshmen. I didn't know the difference between Catholic and Christian. She didn't know which was the bagel and which was the lox. This is true. Our friendship is closing in on fifty years. Sometimes we talk daily, sometimes monthly. It doesn't matter because we pick up the threads of conversation wherever we have left them. Anne and Seth have their special word games. She arranged his art opening at Penn State College of Medicine. She is Seth's friend and advocate. She was the first person to help me with this book.

Lois Rose is my liver. She does for me what I am not strong enough to do for myself. She is inexplicably loyal and available. She shows up whenever she thinks I am housebound, interrupts my solitude, and drives me into the country to buy plants. I go happily. Lois drives Seth to his exhibitions, orchestrates his parties, and takes him for walks. When she walks in, Seth yells, "Party!"

Acknowledgments

Ann Kocks is part of lives. During breakfast, Ann and Seth go over Seth's favorite newspaper articles about construction, new bridges, and roller coasters. Seth will chase Ann down until this happens. She eats with him, helps him get organized in the morning, takes him to museums, movies, theater, and other outings. She is there for him. Ann keeps Seth happy and safe in our home, on field trips, and when we travel. She does what I lack the energy to do. She and her husband, Ken, and their kids have the vision of different generations. We have a richer life with them in it.

Thomas Taxman, MD, is our GI and functional medicine doctor. Tom is dedicated and never gives up. He is a pediatrician. Drawing blood from preemies in the neonatal intensive care unit makes drawing blood from adults a day at the beach. He is the best. When you have an autistic kid, a physician's skill, dedication, and tender touch is what you need for yourself and for your child.

Virginia Shapiro, DC, is uniquely experienced to provide holistic care. I have flown to Duluth, Minnesota, and to Corvallis, Oregon, to get outstanding treatment for myself, my dad, and my son. Since 1999, she has patiently peeled the onion of my medical mysteries.

Ira McEvoy was there for me when Seth was diagnosed. She called often and sent books and chocolate. Later she collected Seth's art. She ordered "the next large horse" before it was started and flew *Cobalt Blue Fantasy Horse* to San Francisco. Ira was willing to wait a year for *Eight Fantasy Griffins over the Rainforest in Costa Rica* and bought three other paintings. Roberta Lowenstein, my cousin, flew in from Aspen, bringing friends to visit us twice and honored us by buying seven of Seth's paintings.

David Baldwin, proprietor of Pancake Pantry, flew in from Nashville three times to buy paintings. People in Ohio call us to say that they were driving their kids to Vanderbilt University, stopped for lunch, and saw Seth's art in Nashville.

Acknowledgments

Jack and Lucy take care of Seth. Jack drives Seth and his art all over town, shopping for Seth's special foods, and taking Seth to museums. He is always pleasant, patient, and smiling, always singing, whistling, or humming. Lucy cooks all of Seth's special foods. She is kind, bright, and creative. Lucy and Jack keep body and soul together. We are so lucky to have them. They are family.

How could it be that Kip Jacobs so recently entered our lives? He is the magician, providing whatever we need. Seth has a studio in Brooklyn, thanks to Kip. He was Seth's mentor in Ghent for three weeks, driving up with enough paint to open a store. "Yes, Seth should paint a decapitation." "Of course Seth can paint *Manhattan Floating*." "Let's measure the lobby of 55 Fifth Avenue, let's see how big he can make it." "Let me read the grant. Have you heard of Jean-Michel Basquiat?" "Seth is my hero. When I watch Seth paint, with all his challenges, he stays so happy, I know I can never complain." "Of course I'll take Seth. Do not worry." Thank you, Kip. I can't say I don't worry, but I worry less.

Then there are the people who support us in the legal and financial world of Seth's autism and the book publishing world. Janet Lowder is our disability lawyer. If I call her before 9 a.m., I can usually reach her that day, which is when I need her. She appreciates and believes in Seth and knows every detail of disability law. Ray Floch is our accountant. His firm took care of my dad when we lived in New York, starting before I was ten. We "inherited" each other. So we live in Cleveland and have an East Coast accountant. He took care of us for fifteen years before we finally met when Seth had an exhibit in New Jersey in June 2009. I don't know what other accountants do, but Ray and the team at GR Reid seem to do a lot. Ray guides us through every step and figures out what to do to meet our needs. There is not much of a template for an artist who happens to be autistic and who paints as therapy for eight years at incredible expense, is not even close to being a business, and yet might suddenly need a financial team.

Faith Hamlin is our literary agent. She took us on in February 2007. I know how people sell books—write an outline, an introduction, and one chapter; get an advance; write a book. I couldn't do it. I couldn't turn the proposal in or trust the project until it was finished. In September 2008, I gave Faith draft number thirty-four, let go, and turned it over to her. It would be unbearable to do this without her. She introduced us to Sheila Curry Oakes, a professional writer with a long history in publishing. Sheila, like a magician, took my words and Seth's paintings, searched for themes, reordered the text, matched the words with the paintings, and transformed the book. As soon as we had a contract with Sterling, we met our editor, Barbara Berger. It is a perfect fit. We bond on every level. Faith then introduced us to Alan Kaufman, our publishing and licensing attorney. We never had one before. He is now part of our life. He is soothing and calming to us and a pit bull in our defense. He is the perfect lawyer.

Seymour Chwast, a distant relative and the most charming of men, responds to all of Seth's e-mails, encourages us, and wrote the preface to this book. Sally Whinnery won Seth's heart. She is a retired special education teacher who works at Cedar Point Amusement Park. She and Seth found each other. Seth calls her daily and truly loves her.

I am grateful for everyone who has access to different realms who helped me. Lynda Yanks, Rabbi David Zeller, and my beloved Kabbalist, Rabbi Yitzchak Schwartz, each made reality shift. I cherish them. I am grateful for the help of the people I depend on. I continue to go forward, leaning on them, still blind, uncertain, dedicated, determined, and doing my best.

Above all, I am grateful for Seth. Every time he walks into the room, my heart fills with joy.

Index of Paintings

Index of Paintings

Index of Paintings

Index of Paintings

Index of Paintings

Index of Paintings

Index of Paintings

About the Authors

DEBRA CHWAST was born in New York City, received a master's in social work from UCLA at Berkeley, and worked as a therapist for thirty-three years. In 1983 she gave birth to her only child, Seth Chwast. When he was diagnosed with autism at twenty-one months, Debra threw herself into an eighteen-year attempt to bring Seth into our world. When a vocational evaluation of Seth recommended a career in dry mopping, Debra stopped working and made creating a life for Seth her full-time job. After Seth discovered painting, Debra produced an eight-minute documentary DVD titled *A Different Kind of Journey*, which was accepted into the Ohio Independent Film Festival in November 2004, featured at Cleveland's Ingenuity Festival of Art and Technology in 2006, and shown on WVIZ PBS many times. It was later seen by the staff of the *Today* show, which led to a feature segment about Seth that aired on January 3, 2007. Debra is now Seth's manager, travel agent, promoter, and—literally—his voice.

At many of Seth's gallery events, Debra speaks to large groups, participates in panels, and provides keynote addresses about her life with Seth.

Now Seth takes Debra into his world, which is one of beauty, joy, and bliss. Debra says, "Seth created me, he catapulted me into endurance, perseverance, creativity, problem-solving, and service. We live an unexpected life, a better life, a life of no limits."

SETH CHWAST, who was diagnosed with autism as a very young child, lived for years in a world of roller coasters, haunted houses, and classical music. A dramatic change came in 2003, when at age twenty he took an oil painting class at the Cleveland Museum of Art. Seth, who rarely speaks, began describing his world in paint. He displayed an innate ability to mix colors and create amazing works of art that reflect his vision of his world and the world around him.

Seth's passions include "making people feel all better," travel, finding the new friends who are everywhere, and Manhattan. Seth's dreams lead to paintings and exhibitions. He has opened at Penn State College of Medicine, University Hospitals of Case Western Reserve University, and the Cleveland Clinic. He has done the cover art for three medical texts. His love of travel has led to exhibitions in Galapagos and the National Gallery of the Cayman Islands, Gulfstream paintings for Trinidad and Tobago, and dolphin paintings for Curaçao. Seth, who loves people and wants to meet everybody, has been on the *Today* show twice, as well as on NPR and PBS. He has exhibited at the United Nations. He has been featured in two documentaries. Having grown up in museums, Seth was thrilled to open in the Cleveland Museum of Natural History and looks forward to his next exhibition there in 2012. He is scheduled for Dartmouth, Curaçao, and Kiev. The man who loves Manhattan is painting regularly in the Brooklyn studio of Kip Jacobs. His fifteen-month painting project, *Manhattan Floating*, opened at Time Equities, Inc. at 55 Fifth Avenue.

Debra and Seth live in Cleveland Heights, Ohio.

Please visit Seth's website at www.SethChwastArt.com.

About the Authors

A Note on the Production

The body text in *An Unexpected Life* is Adobe Jenson Pro. This is an elegant serif typeface created in 1995 for Adobe by American type designer Robert Slimbach, who based it on a Venetian text face cut by French engraver, printer, and typo designer Nicolas Jenson in 1470. Its italics are based on those by early sixteenth-century Italian type designer Ludovico Vicentino degli Arrighi.

The display fonts for directionals and chapter numbers are the art deco-inspired Clichee, designed in 1994 by Czech designer František Štorm.

The chapter titles were drawn by hand especially for this book by Seth Chwast.

Printed and bound by 1010 Printing International Ltd., in China.